Reflections

through Timeless Service:

Alpha Kappa Alpha Sorority, Incorporated

Phi Epsilon Omega Chapter

Authors

Daneen W. Edmond
Charlesnika T. Evans
Tamara McClain
Cindy N. Sanders
Germayne Cade

ISBN-13: 978-0615962092

ISBN-10: 0615962092

Library of Congress Control Number: 201490109

Contents

ACKNOWLEDGMENTS

The authors would like to thank the charter members of Phi Epsilon Omega chapter for their vision and all members of the chapter throughout the years for their dedication. Without your service 'through the years', there would be no Phi Epsilon Omega.

Our interest group would never have been chartered as Phi Epsilon Omega chapter without the support of 24th Central Regional Director Soror Peggy Lewis LeCompte and 25th Central Regional Director Soror Nadine C. Bonds. Without assistance and appointments from the 26th Central Regional Director Soror Dorothy Buckhanan Wilson, 27th Central Regional Director Soror Pamela Bates Porch, and 28th Central Regional Director Soror Giselé M. Casanova, our chapter would never have blossomed.

Soror Yolanda Talley (chapter historian 2013-2014) kept the authors on task by organizing meetings, attending Timeless History workshops, and providing up-to-date resources on necessary inclusion items for the submission. Without Soror Yolanda's input, this history book might not have been completed in an acceptable manner. The authors would also like to thank Sorors Timeka Gee and Shawanda Jennings for their aid in providing resources to accurately document Phi Epsilon Omega chapter's history. The authors are especially grateful to Soror LaTonya Gunter for editing this history and Soror Dianne Wolfe for the cover design.

ALPHA KAPPA ALPHA SORORITY, INCORPORATED

A Legacy of Sisterhood and Timeless Service

Confined to what she called "a small circumscribed life" in the segregated and male-dominated milieu that characterized the early 1900s, Howard University co-ed Ethel Hedgeman dreamed of creating a support network for women with like minds coming together for mutual uplift, and coalescing their talents and strengths for the benefit of others. In 1908, her vision crystallized as Alpha Kappa Alpha, the first Negro Greek-letter sorority. Five years later (1913), lead incorporator Nellie Quander ensured Alpha Kappa Alpha's perpetuity through incorporation in the District of Columbia.

Together with eight other coeds at the mecca for Negro education, Hedgeman crafted a design that not only fostered interaction, stimulation, and ethical growth among members; but also provided hope for the masses. From the core group of nine at Howard, AKA has grown into a force of more than 265,000 collegiate members and alumnae, constituting 972 chapters in 42 states, the District of Columbia, the US Virgin Islands, the Bahamas, Germany, South Korea, Japan, Liberia, and Canada.

Because they believed that Negro college women represented "the highest—more education, more enlightenment, and more of almost everything that the great mass of Negroes never had— Hedgeman and her cohorts worked to honor what she called "an everlasting debt to raise them (Negroes) up and to make them better." For more than a century, the Alpha Kappa Alpha Sisterhood has fulfilled that obligation by becoming an indomitable force for good in their communities, state, nation, and the world.

The Alpha Kappa Alpha program today still reflects the communal consciousness steeped in the AKA tradition and embodied in AKA's credo, "To be supreme in service to all mankind." Cultural awareness and social advocacy marked Alpha Kappa Alpha's infancy, but within one year (1914) of acquiring corporate status, AKA had also made its mark on education, establishing a scholarship award. The programming was a prelude to the thousands of pioneering and enduring initiatives that eventually defined the Alpha Kappa Alpha brand.

Through the years, Alpha Kappa Alpha has used the Sisterhood as a grand lever to raise the status of African-Americans, particularly girls and women. AKA has enriched minds and encouraged life-long learning; provided aid for the poor, the sick, and underserved; initiated social action to advance human and civil rights; worked collaboratively with other groups to maximize outreach on progressive endeavors; and continually produced leaders to continue its credo of service.

Guided by twenty-eight international presidents from Nellie M. Quander (1913-1919) to Carolyn House Stewart (2010-2014), with reinforcement from a professional headquarters staff since 1949; AKA's corps of volunteers has instituted groundbreaking social action initiatives and social service programs that have timelessly transformed communities for the better—continually emitting progress in cities, states, the nation, and the world.

Signal Program Initiatives

2000s—Launched Emerging Young Leaders, a bold move to prepare 10,000 girls in grades 6-8 to excel as young leaders equipped to respond to the challenges of the 21st century; initiated homage for civil rights milestones by honoring the Little Rock Nine's 1957 desegregation of Central High (Little Rock, Ar.) following the Supreme Court's 1954 decision declaring segregated schools unconstitutional; donated $1 million to Howard University to fund scholarships and preserve Black culture (2008); strengthened the reading skills of 16,000 children through a $1.5 million after school demonstration project in low-performing, economically deprived, inner city schools (2002); and improved the quality of life for people of African descent through continuation of aid to African countries.

1990s—Built 10 schools in South Africa (1998); added the largest number of minorities to the National Bone Marrow Registry (1996); Became first civilian organization to create memorial to World War II unsung hero Dorie Miller (1991).

1980s—Adopted more than 27 African villages, earning Africare's 1986 Distinguished Service Award; encouraged awareness of and participation in the nation's affairs, registering more than 350, 000 new voters; and established the Alpha Kappa Alpha Educational Advancement Foundation (1981), a multimillion dollar entity that annually awards more than $100,000 in scholarships, grants, and fellowships.

1970's— Was only sorority to be named an inaugural member of Operation Big Vote (1979); completed pledge of one-half million to the United Negro College Fund (1976); and purchased Dr. Martin Luther King's boyhood home for the MLK Center for Social Change (1972).

1960s—Sponsored inaugural Domestic Travel Tour, a one-week cultural excursion for 30 high school students (1969); launched a "Heritage Series" on African-American achievers (1965); and emerged as the first women's group to win a grant to operate a federal job corps center (1965), preparing youth 16-21 to function in a highly competitive economy.

1950s—Promoted investing in Black businesses by depositing initial $38,000 for AKA

Investment Fund with the first and only Negro firm on Wall Street (1958). Spurred Sickle Cell Disease research and education with grants to Howard Hospital and publication of *The Sickle Cell Story* (1958).

1940s—Invited other Greek-letter organizations to come together to establish the American Council on Human Rights to empower racial uplift and economic development (1948); Acquired observer status from the United Nations (1946); and challenged the absence of people of color from pictorial images used by the government to portray Americans (1944).

1930s—Became first organization to take out NAACP life membership (1939); Created nation's first Congressional lobby that impacted legislation on issues ranging from decent living conditions and jobs to lynching (1938); and established the nation's first mobile health clinic, providing relief to 15,000 Negroes plagued by famine and disease in the Mississippi Delta (1935).

1920s—Worked to dispel notions that Negroes were unfit for certain professions, and guided Negroes in avoiding career mistakes (1923); pushed anti-lynching legislation (1921).

1900s—Promoted Negro culture and encouraged social action through presentation of Negro artists and social justice advocates, including elocutionist Nathaniel Guy, Hull House founder Jane Addams, and U. S. Congressman Martin Madden (1908-1915). Established the first organizational scholarship at Howard University (1914).

—Earnestine Green McNealey, Ph.D., AKA Historian

August 2013

ALPHA KAPPA ALPHA SORORITY, INCORPORATED

THE HISTORY OF CENTRAL REGION - "PLEDGED TO REMEMBER"

A TRADITION OF TIMELESS SERVICE

It takes only one drop of water to start a waterfall and so it was with the building of the organizational structure of Alpha Kappa Alpha Sorority, Incorporated. Thus, the idea of one molded by nine, nurtured by sixteen, and incorporated by three spawned the evolution of this great sisterhood.

Following the sorority's incorporation in 1913 and the election of the first Supreme Basileus, Nellie Quander, the sorority began its expansion beyond Howard University. Quander appointed the first national organizer, Founder Beulah Elizabeth Burke to help with the expansion. Founder Burke moved swiftly in her task and chartered Beta Chapter in Chicago, IL on October 8, 1913 giving Beta Chapter the distinction of being the first chapter chartered following the sorority's incorporation. Beta Chapter's chartering was soon followed by the chartering of Gamma Chapter at the University of Illinois Urbana-Champaign on February 12, 1914 (the first chapter chartered on a predominately White campus). The chartering of these two chapters was the beginning of the legacy of Central Region and its members roles and contributions to the growth and development of Alpha Kappa Alpha Sorority, Incorporated.

During the sorority's early years, chapters were not designated according to regions however, a regional structure was inevitable. The first indication of this was the addition of geographic designations to the titles of the National Organizers (the first title of Regional Directors) which occurred following the 2nd Boule when a Central, Western, and Eastern Organizer were appointed. Six years later, at the eighth Boule in 1925, the title Regional Director was officially adopted and seven regions were established: Northeastern, Eastern, Southeastern, Central, Southern, Central Western and Western. Central Region was comprised of the states of Ohio, Michigan, Wisconsin, Illinois, and Indiana. At the ninth Boule in 1926 Central Region's name would be changed to the North Central Region and Kentucky would briefly become a part of the North Central Region. The sorority once again reorganized the chapters of Alpha Kappa Alpha at the 11th Boule in 1928 and North Central Region would again become Central Region and Minnesota would return to the Region.

Many changes have occurred in the name designation of regions and the states comprising those regions. The exact date of the current composition of Central Region (Illinois, Indiana, Kentucky, Minnesota, St. Louis and Cape Girardeau, Missouri, Wisconsin, and North and South Dakota) could not be pinpointed. However, Gamma Omega in St. Louis became a part of Central Region with the election of Blanche Hayes Clark as Central Regional Director due to the requirement adopted by the Boule in 1930 that the Regional Director must reside in the region from which she is elected. The state of Kentucky rejoined Central Region by 1956 and North and South Dakota joined in 1964; and Cape Girardeau, Missouri joined the region with the chartering of Nu Sigma Chapter, Southeastern Missouri State University, on March 22, 1981.

Historically, leading the way has been the hallmark of Central Region beginning with the election of the second Supreme Basileus of the sorority Loraine Richardson Green in 1919 at the 2nd Boule in Chicago, IL. Also elected at that Boule were Pauline Kigh Reed, Central and Western Organizer, and from Indianapolis, Indiana, Murray B. Atkins, Assistant Grammateus, Phyllis Wheatley Waters, Supreme Epistoleus and Myrtle Johnson, Assistant Epistoleus.

During her term as Supreme Basileus 1920-1923 Loraine Green presided at four Boules and the sorority's operational structure began to take shape. The Constitution of the Boule of Alpha Kappa Alpha Sorority (the original name of the document) was adopted; membership and other official forms were created; the first Ivy Leaf was published; the Coat of Arms designed by Phyllis Wheatley Waters of Indianapolis, IN was adopted; and the annual National Founders' Day observance was established. In 1926 Alpha Eta Omega Chapter charter member Evangeline Harris Merriweather wrote the words and music to the Ivy Hymn and according to historical papers housed in the Virgo County Public Library, Terre Haute, IN she also wrote the words to the Initiation Hymn.

The regional structure of the sorority has served to help with the administration of chapters and program implementation. Organizing chapters and oversight of chapter operations and programs were under the jurisdiction of National Organizers until 1925. Pauline Kigh Reed, December 1919 - December 1922, Fredericka Brown December 1922 - December 1923, and Carolynne Payne, December 1923 - December 1925 served as Central Organizers. Murray B. Atkins was the first soror to be elected with the title Central Regional Director. She served from December 1925 - December 1927 followed by Althea M. Simmons December 1927 - December 1930.

Since the first Central Regional Conference in 1931, the Region has grown from nine chapters (five Undergraduate and four Graduate Chapters) and approximately 100 recorded members in 1931 to in 2013 ninety chapters (53 Graduate Chapters and 37 Undergraduate Chapters) with an active membership of 3,899 (3,509 Graduate members and 390 Undergraduate members). And has been expertly led by twenty-three Directors who have presided over 79 Central Regional Conferences: Blanche Hayes Clark, December 1930 - December 1934; Alice McGhee Smart, December 1934 - December 1937; Arlene J. Washington, December 1937 - December 1940; Blanche L. Patterson McWilliams, December 1940 - December 1943; Maenell Hamlin Newsome, December 1943 - August 1946; Lucille Wilkins, August 1946 - December 1950; Evelyn Roberts, December 1950 - December 1954; Maude L. Mann, December 1954 - August 1958; Annetta M. Lawson, August 1958 - December 1962; Lee Anna Shelburne, December 1962 - August 1966; Ordie Amelia Roberts, August 1966 - August 1970; Johnetta Randolph Haley, August 1970 - August 1974; Gloria E. Smith Bond, August 1974 - July 1978; Peggy Jean Lewis LeCompte, July 1978 - July 1982; Mable Evans Cason, July 1982 - July 1986; Loann J. Honesty King, July 1986 - July 1990; Yvonne Perkins, July 1990 - July 1994; Martha Levingston Perine, July 1994 – 1997; Peggy Lewis LeCompte, 1997-1998; Nadine Bonds, 1998-2002; Dorothy

Wilson Buckhanan, 2002-2006; Pamela Bates Porch, 2006-2010; and Giselé M. Casanova, 2010–2014.

Central Region is proud of its history over the past ten decades and the service rendered by its members who have served at every level in Alpha Kappa Alpha Sorority. Four have served as Supreme Basileus: Loraine Richardson Green (2nd), 1918-1923; Maudelle Brown Bousfield (6th), 1929-1931; Maude Brown Porter (7th), 1931-1933; Linda Marie White (26th) and Dorothy Buckhanan Wilson will become the 29th Supreme Basileus in 2014.

Six members have served as First Supreme Anti-Basileus: Zelma Watson, Carolynne Payne, Maudelle Brown Bousfield, Maude Brown Porter, Lucile Robinson Wilkins, Linda Marie White and currently Dorothy Buckhanan Wilson; two have been elected Second Supreme Anti-Basileus; Frances E. Smith, Nan Arrington Peete; three Undergraduate Members-at-Large: Erica S. Horton, Delta Springer Irby, Anita L. McCollum (Irby and McCollum were attending schools outside of the region when elected); nine as Supreme Grammateus: Irma Frazier Clarke, Elizabeth Johnson, Carolyn S. Blanton, Murray B, Atkins (Walls), Evelyn H. Roberts, Lauretta Naylor Thompson, Peggy Lewis LeCompte, Linda Marie White and Dorothy Buckhanan Wilson; eight as Supreme Tamiouchos: Irma Frazier Clarke, Gladys Buffin Johnson, Helen Cromer Cooper, Loann J. Honesty King, Yvonne Perkins (two terms), Martha Levingston Perine and Barbara A. McKinzie; five Supreme Parliamentarians: Lucille B. Wilkins, Gladys Chapman Gordon, Helen Cromer Cooper, Johnetta Randolph Haley and Constance Kinard Holland; one International Regional Director: Nadine Bonds.

The 48th Boule established the current size and composition of the Directorate in July 1978. This action abolished several offices from the Directorate structure. Also, the Boule dissolved the executive committee and the public relations committee and enlarged the constitution committee and program committee to include representation from each region. Central Region members who served in these positions were: Supreme Anti-Grammateus, Murray B. Atkins; Supreme Epistoleus: Phyllis Waters, Alice McGhee Smart, and Irma Frazier Clarke; Financial Director: Helen Cromer Cooper and Lauretta Naylor Thompson; Editor-in-Chief of the Ivy Leaf: Helen Kathleen Perry (1st), Althea Merchant Simmons and C. Elizabeth Johnson; Director of Publicity: Bertha Moseley Lewis and Pauline Kigh Reed; Undergraduate Program Advisor: Hazel Ross Bolan; and Graduate Member-at-Large: Lauretta Naylor Thompson.

National/International Standing Committees have been chaired by: Constitution: Helen Cromer Cooper, Constance Kinard Holland and Johnetta R. Haley; Finance: Helen Cromer Cooper, Lauretta Naylor Thompson, Loann J. Honesty King, Barbara A. McKinzie, Martha Perine Beard and Yvonne Perkins; Program: Marian J. Warring and Loann J. Honesty King; Nominating (elected): Beatrice Lafferty Murphy, Constance Kinard Holland and Giselé Casanova; Building and Properties: Alison Harris Alexander and Carey Preston; Personnel/Human Resources (1990) Nan E. McGehee, Helen Cromer Cooper, Evelyn Freeman Walker, Gloria E. Bond, and Deborah Hill Burroughs; Membership: Peggy Lewis LeCompte and Alana M. Broady; Standards: Leola Madison, Johnetta Randolph Haley and Yvonne Perkins; Honorary Members and Rewards: Mae Ruth Carr; and Technology: Brenda Ladipo.

In addition, to chairing standing committees Central Region Members have provided extraordinary service as members of these committees as well as on other committees with at least twenty having served in multiple elected or appointed positions. It should also be noted that the position of Supreme Tamiouchos was held by Central Region members for sixteen consecutive years 1986-2002.

Several Central Region members have also served in special appointed capacities. In 1990 Alana M. Broady and Linda M. White were appointed the first Protocol Liaisons and Larnell Burks Bagley also served in the position. Barbara A. McKinzie chaired the first Business Roundtable Committee and Loann J. Honesty King; Chairman of the Economic Development Sub-Committee chaired the sorority's first Economic Development Conference in 1983,Washington, D.C. Mae Ruth Carr was personal escort to Honorary Member Madame Leah Tutu at the 52nd Boule in 1986.

The Centennial Traveling Exhibit was conceptualized and developed by June Mustifield and Audrey Cooper-Stanton has led the Leadership Fellows Program as Chairman of the committee from 2006 – 2014. Essie Blaylock (2002-2006) and Ericka V. Everett (2006-2009) served as Executive Assistant to the Supreme Basileus. Other Central Region members who received Special Chairman Appointments were Rita Wilson, Corporate Partnership/Marketing; Peggy Lewis LeCompte, Central Region Heritage Committee; Melody McDowell, Communications Committee and Yvonne Perkins, Graduate/Undergraduate Concerns.

Nine Central Region members have received The Founders' Graduate Service Award (the sorority's highest honor given to a member) for their outstanding record of service to Alpha Kappa Alpha and the community. They are Helen Cromer Cooper, Delta Chi Omega; Winona Lee Fletcher, Kappa Tau Omega; Constance Kinard Holland, Kappa Tau Omega; Frances Brock Starms, Epsilon Kappa Omega; Johnetta Randolph Haley, Omicron Theta Omega; Nadine C. Bonds, Alpha Mu Omega; Loann J. Honesty King, Theta Omega; Peggy Lewis LeCompte, Delta Delta Omega and Audrey Cooper-Stanton, Theta Omega. The region is also home to eight honorary members including the sorority's first honorary member, Chicago's Hull House founder Jane Addams.

Central Region can boast of being the home to the sorority's Corporate Office and its members have served in advisory and volunteer roles from the opening of the first office on October 8, 1949 in Chicago, IL to the purchase of the first property at 5211 South Greenwood in 1951 to the multimillion dollar facility at 5656 S. Stony Island Avenue. Four of the ten Executive Directors have come from Central Region: Carey B. Maddox Preston, Barbara A. McKinzie, Alison A. Harris Alexander and Deborah L. Dangerfield. The street in front of the Corporate Office bears the honorary name of Loraine Richardson Green Drive because of the efforts of member Doris Powell.

The Corporate Office also houses the Educational Advancement Foundation (EAF) created in 1980 to ensure perpetual support for its commitment to education. Central Region's Constance Kinard Holland, Kappa Tau Omega Chapter was the visionary and conceptual drafter of EAF, drafted the articles of incorporation and served as a Member-at-Large on the 1st elected Board of Directors. Peggy Lewis LeCompte, Delta Delta Omega Chapter served as Secretary and Challis M. Lowe, Theta Omega Chapter as Member-at-Large also served on the 1st elected Board of Directors; Loann J. Honesty King, Theta Omega Chapter, was an incorporator and the first Treasurer. Doris Parker, Alpha Mu Omega, was appointed the EAF's first Executive Secretary and Central Region members Deborah Dangerfield and Barbara Sutton both from Theta Omega Chapter served as Executive Director.

Central Region has also hosted:

> Eleven Boules including the second in 1919, Silver Anniversary Boule, 1944 and the last Boule of the twentieth century, 1998
> Four Leadership Conferences: 1981 in Indianapolis, and 1983, 1985, and 1991 in Chicago, IL
> The first national reading experience workshop in Chicago, with Theta Omega Chapter as organizers.
> The first Leadership Fellows program in Spencer, IN near Bloomington at the McCormick Creek State Park in 1976.
> The 17th and 18th Leadership Fellows program in Minneapolis, MN in 1997 and 1998 respectively at the Sheraton Minneapolis Metro dome in partnership with Pillsbury.

Commitment, dedication, and loyalty to the sisterhood are continually exhibited by Central Region members. As a whole, the members of the Central Region have never failed to rise to the occasion or answer the call, and often go beyond the expected. As we look to the future the Confident Central Region members remain prepared to continue to carry and pass on the torch in "Service to All Mankind."

Loann Julia Honesty King, Central Region Historian

September 2013

CHARTERING:

FROM THE ULTIMATE WOMEN OF PINK AND GREEN TO

THE SORORS OF PHI EPSILON OMEGA CHAPTER

In November 1997, several members of Alpha Kappa Alpha Sorority, Incorporated met to discuss the chartering of a new graduate chapter of Alpha Kappa Alpha Sorority in the Chicago area. They wanted to use their time and talents to better serve the community and the Sorority. On November 16, 1997, this group of women named themselves "The Ultimate Women of Pink and Green". Under the leadership of Bakahia Madison, the group's membership increased to nineteen members.

The officers of the Ultimate Women of Pink and Green Interest Group were Bakahia Madison (President), Tina Roberson (Vice President), U. Schanee Woods (Recording Secretary), Germayne Smith (Corresponding Secretary), Tanya Foucher (Treasurer), Marsha L. Golliday (Membership Chairman), Desirie Howard (Hostess), Anjanette Ivy (Fundraising Chairman), Cindy N. Sanders (Historian/Ivy Leaf Reporter), Sharice Fox (Communication Chairman), Theresa Andrews (Bylaws Chairman), and LaTonya Gunter (Sergeant-at-Arms).

Over the next year, the interest group continued to meet and develop programs for the community in Health and Education. The Ultimate Women did many service projects including grading entrance exams for a local high school, organizing and staffing "Healthy Kids Day" at the South Side YMCA, conducting the "Positive Black Women" presentation for girls from age 12-18 at the Burnham Girls Group Home, and providing a skating party for the cheerleaders and basketball team at Martin L. King elementary school in Dixmoor, IL for winning first place in district. The interest group also held a health and beauty seminar and a Black Family Market, which were both well attended and well received by the community. By mid-1998, the interest group members began taking steps to initiate the chartering process; their tremendous efforts proved fruitful.

The Ultimate Women of Pink and Green Interest Group was chartered as Phi Epsilon Omega Chapter on January 23, 1999 in Harvey, Illinois. The chartering ceremony took place at the Best Western in Homewood, Illinois. The 25th Central Regional Director, Soror Nadine C. Bonds, conducted the ceremony. The 25th Supreme Basileus, Soror Norma S. White, and the 25th Supreme Tamiouchos, Soror Barbara A. McKinzie, also attended the chartering celebration.

Seated l to r: 25th Supreme Tamiouchos Soror Barbara A. McKinzie, 25th Supreme Basileus Soror Norma S. White, 25th Central Regional Director Soror Nadine C. Bonds, Standing: Soror Alfreda K. Keller

21

The charter members of Phi Epsilon Omega chapter are:

NISA (LISA) JOHNSON
THERESA ANDREWS
NATASHA BUCKNER
DANEEN WOODARD
EDMOND
TANYA FOUCHER
MARSHA L. GOLLIDAY
LATONYA A. GUNTER
DESIRIE K. HOWARD
ANJANETTE IVY
LISA JOE

SHARICE MCCANTS-
FOX
DETRA C. MCCLARITY
TANYA MCCRAY
BAKAHIA REED-
MADISON
TINA C. ROBERSON
CINDY N. SANDERS
GERMAYNE L. SMITH
U. SCHANEE WOODS
EBONI ZAMANI

Charter Members with 25th Central Regional Director Soror Nadine C. Bonds
Not pictured: Soror U. Schanee Woods and Soror Eboni (Zamani) Gallaher

MEMBERSHIP TIMELINE

Motivated by the chartering of the new chapter, several sorors reactivated through the chapter soon after its chartering. They were: Charlotte Curtis, Denedra Givens-Ellis, Heather Holland, Narissa Jones, LaTacia Morgan-Greene, Angela Murray, Antoinette Patton, Timeka Patton Gee, and LaTisha Robinson Bell.

This new chapter decided to expand its sisterhood even further by conducting its first membership intake process. The first initiation ceremony of the chapter was held May 7, 2000 at the Best Western in Homewood, Illinois. The first initiates included: Cara Alley, Yolanda Anthony, Toya Supreme, Sabrina Butler, Cleopatra Cowley, Marie Davis, LaKeisha Grace-Stewart, Ingrid Jones, Charlesnika Evans, Shayla Maatuka, Breian Meakens, Danielle Mitchell, Tamiko Mitchell, Lisa Moore, Shivonne Nelson, Keiana Peyton, Ayanna Perkins, Terrycita Perry, Dawn Phillips, Traci Powell, LaKeisha Ross, Deana Sanders, Rachel Rowell, Erika Simmons, Celeste Smith, Toi Walker, Kimberly White, and Cynette Wilson.

New sorors of Phi Epsilon Omega chapter at luncheon after 1st initiation

The second initiation ceremony was held April 7, 2002 at the Radisson Hotel in Merrillville, Indiana and included: Catrice Armstrong, Bridgett F. Earls, Valencia Jones, Nikki Laury, Kamita Terrell, Katrina Terrell, and Sukari Washington.

New sorors of Phi Epsilon Omega chapter at luncheon after 2nd initiation in 2002

.

Soror Tamara McClain and Soror Tonya Weatherly transferred into Phi Epsilon Omega chapter in January 2004. Soror Natasha Rochelle transferred from Zeta Iota into Phi Epsilon Omega in 2005.

The third initiation ceremony was held February 26, 2006 at the Oak Brook Marriott in Oak Brook, Illinois and included: Sorors Margo Anderson, De'Onna Cavin, Leah Humphrey, Tiffany Majors, Patrice McCoy, Michelle Rainey, Michelle Ross, Antoinette Weston, Erika Whitehead, Ceshia Wilder, Attiyya Williams, and Kim Willis.

New sorors at luncheon after 3rd initiation ceremony in 2006. Pictured with Sorors K. Peyton and T. Gee.

In 2007 Sorors Shawanda Jennings, Vanessa Johnson, and Sandra Rush-Atkins were welcomed into Phi Epsilon Omega chapter along with reactivated/transfer Sorors Toya L. Campbell and Tanya Stephens-Berry. Sorors Lori Burns and Heather Duncan Whitt reactivated in 2008. Soror Nicole Spicer reactivated in 2010 after relocating back to the Chicagoland area from Georgia.

After Soror Hareder McDowell reactivated with the sorority in 2010, she encouraged inactive sorors from Zeta Iota chapter to attend chapter meetings. Many of whom subsequently reactivated between the years of 2011 and 2014: Sorors Dana Stafford-Menefee, Danielle Graham-Harris, Barbara Martin, Alicia Mattocks, Ursula Burns, Tammy Scott-Brand, Christine Chambers, Dana Woods, Sherry Randall-Hardin, Shawn L. Govan, and Rhea Henderson have returned to Alpha Kappa Alpha Sorority, Inc. and the sorors of Phi Epsilon Omega chapter.

In 2013, Soror Marian Dozier and Soror Maji Tharpe reactivated with Phi Epsilon Omega chapter.

The fifth membership initiation ceremony was held September 29, 2013 at the Holiday Inn Convention Center in Tinley Park, IL. The initiates included Soror Javanese Byrd, Soror Brittany McGhee, Soror Catherine Amy Moy, Soror Jeanne Pierce, Soror Trina Robinson, Soror Amissah Lemieux-Seals, Soror Monica Renee Shirley, and Soror Dianne Wolfe.

New sorors at luncheon after 5th initiation ceremony in 2013. Pictured with chapter officers.

Zeta Iota chapter at Western Illinois University was in danger of being dissolved when Phi Epsilon Omega chapter became its supervising graduate chapter in 2001. As this chapter is 3 hours from the Chicago land area, previous graduate advisors Sorors Timeka Gee, Cindy Sanders, Bakahia Madison, Sharice Fox, and current graduate advisor Soror Barbara Martin have spent numerous hours on the road to revitalize, guide, and supervise this chapter. The first membership intake process (MIP) under the supervision of Phi Epsilon Omega chapter was held in the fall of 2001. The last MIP in 2013 provided Zeta Iota chapter with 25 new sorors. Zeta Iota has joint chapter meetings with Phi Epsilon Omega chapter in May and December of each year.

2001 Zeta Iota initiates with Phi Epsilon Omega sorors

Since the chapter's chartering, Phi Epsilon Omega's average membership has been about 35 sorors. Due to the diligence of membership chairman, Soror Charlesnika Evans, the chapter reached Pearl level for membership in 2006. Soror Charlesnika held many retention and reactivation efforts throughout her 4 years as membership chairman. She and the membership committee sent mailings, decorated inactive sorors' front doors, and coordinated numerous special events.

At the end of 2013, Phi Epsilon Omega chapter had a membership of 50 active sorors. Two additional inactive sorors paid dues for 2014 at the December 2013 meeting with another 5 sorors transferring into the chapter early January 2014. With the continuous efforts of our current membership chairman, Soror Detra McClarity Reynolds, and her committee, Phi Epsilon Omega chapter is forging away to increase this sisterhood to new heights

CHAPTER LEADERSHIP

Bakahia Madison
Basileus 1999-2000

Soror Bakahia Madison is one amazing soror. She is a wife, mother of one son, and the founder of the Coalition for Family Based Treatment and she still finds the time to assist with the sorority. She is not only a charter member of Phi Epsilon Omega chapter; she is the driving force for its existence. She worked tirelessly for years as the president of the Ultimate Women of Pink and Green Interest Group to bring together a group of sorors that would not only serve the Harvey/Dixmoor communities, but would work well together as sisters. She is an extremely passionate person who had a vision for a chapter and over a decade later still reminds sorors of this vision. She was initiated into Alpha Kappa Alpha Sorority in the fall of 1991 via Zeta Iota chapter.

Soror Bakahia has served the chapter in numerous positions. She was an excellent Basileus (1999-2000), but serving four years as Graduate Advisor (2003-2006) to an undergraduate chapter 3 hours away was an amazing and selfless feat. She has also held the offices of 2nd Anti-basileus (2002), Standards Chairman (2001-2002), Parliamentarian (2001-2002, 2011-2012), and Historian (2007-2008). She has also been on the Central Region's Technology committee (2006-2010), the chairman of the workshops committee for the 68th Central Regional Conference, the chairman of the Philacters committee for the 66th and 67th Central Regional Conference, the co-chairman (2003) and chairman (2004) of the Joint Founders' Day Celebration committee, and one of the general chairmen (2009) of the 75th Central Regional Conference. Soror Bakahia is at almost every chapter meeting, program, chapter social event, and every soror's baby shower, bridal shower, wedding, birthday party, etc. She shows the chapter what being in this sorority truly means. Because of this, the chapter awarded her with the title Soror of the Year in 2000 and Unsung Shero of the Year for 2007.

Soror Madison has a Bachelor's degree in Psychology, a Master's degree in Community Mental Health Counseling, and a PsyD in Clinical Psychology. Her career truly allows her to alleviate problems concerning girls and women and to serve all mankind. In her previous position as Director for Women and Children Services for Haymarket Center, she provided programs for the clients at the center and brought in the chapter to assist in numerous ways. The chapter has participated in their Black History Month Celebration and coordinated programs for Black males providing information on health, legal issues, and finances.

Soror Madison also chartered a chapter of the Rebecca Project for Human Rights (a legal and advocacy organization for low-income women and their families struggling with the intersecting issues of economic marginality, substance abuse, access to family-oriented treatment, and the criminal justice system). As Soror Bakahia provided sorors access to Haymarket Center for programs, the Rebecca Project likely will be another avenue for Phi Epsilon Omega to serve.

Anjanette Ivy Johnson
Basileus 2001-2002

Soror Anjanette Ivy Johnson (Basileus 2001-2002) is a charter member of Phi Epsilon Omega chapter. She was the corresponding secretary for the Ultimate Women of Pink and Green interest group. She also held the position of Grammateus (1999-2000) for Phi Epsilon Omega Chapter. She was our soror who Blazed New Trails. Soror Anjanette emphasized sisterhood during her time as Basileus. The inaugural chapter retreat commenced under Soror Anjanette's leadership. The impact of this retreat was profound because it enabled sorors to gather collectively to review the prior months and prepare for the future with the reconvening of chapter business in September. Chapter officers and duties were reviewed and the office of 2nd Anti-Basileus was created at this retreat. The vision of our chapter was created during her administration at the chapter's executive committee retreat and is as follows:

The vision of Alpha Kappa Alpha Sorority, Incorporated, Phi Epsilon Omega chapter

is to foster the unbreakable bonds of sisterhood from within and to service the Harvey community through programs, mentoring, and volunteering.

Soror Anjanette was initiated into Alpha Kappa Alpha Sorority, Incorporated into Zeta Iota chapter in 1991. She is married and the mother of 2 children. She is currently the Metro Market Manager for Robert Half Internationals Midtown & Galleria offices in Atlanta, Georgia.

Anjanette Johnson has more than 15 years of experience in recruiting, conducting interviews and making final hiring decisions. Soror Anjanette has experience working with S&P 500 Index and Fortune 500 Companies across many industries to ensure their success in this area. She has been responsible for the acquisition of top talent in the areas of: Accounting, Sales, Administrative/Office Support, Nursing and other specialty areas. Soror Johnson has also worked in the post-secondary education arena holding workshops to assist with ensuring students are prepared for success after graduation.

Marsha L. Golliday
Interim Basileus November/December 2002

When Soror Johnson moved to Georgia 2 months before the end of her term, Soror Marsha L. Golliday became interim

Basileus. Soror Marsha has held the offices of Parliamentarian (2007-2008), Membership Chairman (early 1999), Philacter (2011-2012), and 1st Anti-Basileus (1999-2002).

Soror Marsha was initiated into Zeta Iota chapter in the fall of 1991. She is married and works as a human resources professional.

Tanya Foucher-Weekley
Basileus 2003-2004

Since her spring 1991 initiation into the Zeta Iota undergraduate chapter at Western Illinois University, Soror Tanya Foucher-Weekley has remained a dedicated and committed community service advocate, mentor, and visionary to her chapter and beyond. Soror Tanya received her bachelor's degree in Chemistry magna cum laude. She also has a master's degree in Accountancy and is a CPA and CFE. She is well regarded amongst her colleagues as a financial professional, maintains a private tax and accounting practice, and works as comptroller for the Public Building Commission of Chicago. Soror Tanya also has operated her own independent tax and accounting practice for the past 15 years and is married and the mother of 1 son.

Soror Tanya Foucher-Weekley (Basileus 2003-2004) is a charter member of Phi Epsilon Omega chapter. She was the Treasurer for the interest group and held the position of Tamiouchos for 4 years (1999-2002). Within the chapter, she has also held the positions of Grammateus (2005-2006), "Shades of

Pink" Cotillion Chairman (2013-2014), Cotillion Co-chairman (2007-2008), and EAF Captain (2009-2010). In addition, she has conducted many financial workshops through the years for chapter retreats. Regionally, she was co-chairman of the Workshops Committee for the 68th Central Regional Conference and Budget and Finance Chairman for the 75th Central Regional Conference in Schaumburg, IL.

As the chapter's first Tamiouchos, Soror Tanya laid the foundation for the chapter's effective financial procedures and operations. Often times being called frugal by Sorors, she maintained the chapter finances with an iron fist and denied Sorors reimbursements without proper approval and documentation. Since being a graduate soror, she has attended every Central Regional Conference and Boule as a representative of the chapter with the exception of Boule in 2010 when her son was born. Her unwavering support of the chapter has granted her the love and respect of her chapter sorors and resulted in her receiving Phi Epsilon Omega's Soror of the Year award in 2002 and the Unsung Shero of the Year award in 2009.

Daneen W. Edmond
Basileus 2005-2006

As Basileus, Soror Daneen W. Edmond decided to save chapter funds and lead the chapter into the new millennium by emailing the chapter newsletter to sorors. In her administration, Soror Daneen targeted two major areas for chapter expansion – the need for a chapter foundation and a chapter website. The chapter website went live in 2006. The foundation committee was unable to complete the goal of the chapter foundation, but Soror Daneen continued researching and solicited the chapter's support and enough funds to initiate the chapter's endowed fund with EAF in 2011. She consistently encouraged the chapter to participate not just in chapter activities, but in regional and national activities. In her second year as Basileus, she submitted a bid for the chapter to host the 75th Central Regional Conference that was accepted by 27th Central Regional Director Soror Pamela Bates Porch.

Soror Daneen Edmond was initiated into Theta Rho Omega chapter in 1993. She is a charter member of Phi Epsilon Omega chapter. In addition to being Basileus, she has served as Membership Chairman (1999-2002), Grammateus (2003-2004), Standards Chairman (2007-2008, 2011-2012), Parliamentarian

(2007-2008), and Technology Chairman (2013-2014). She has also served on the Central Region's Heritage Committee (2006-2010), as one of the Logistics Chairmen for the 75th Central Regional Conference, as Ivy Leaf Reporter for the Chicagoland Basilei Council (2006), and as a member of the Central Region's Evaluations committee (2010-2014).

Soror Daneen obtained her B.S. in Chemistry from the University of Illinois at Urbana-Champaign. She obtained her M.D. from the Southern Illinois University School of Medicine. Her residency was completed in Internal Medicine and Pediatrics at the University of Illinois at Chicago Medical Center. She is also married and the mother of 2 children.

She is a practicing physician at a not for profit agency that provides quality health care to the underserved populations of Chicago. She is board certified in both Internal Medicine and Pediatrics and serves as a Regional Medical Director and Associate Medical Director for the Utilization Management department at her organization. She is also a preceptor for students enrolled at Rush University and the Rosalind Franklin School of Medical Sciences. She is also certified in EpicCare Ambulatory, one the nation's premier electronic health records.

Soror Daneen was recognized for her achievements by the chapter as Soror of the Year in 2005 and by the Central Region as Outstanding Basileus for 2005 at the 72nd Central Regional Conference.

Timeka Patton Gee
Basileus 2007-2008

In the celebratory year of our 100th year centennial celebration, Soror Timeka Patton Gee served as the Basileus of our chapter. She was initiated into the world of Alpha Kappa Alpha in 1998 through Pi Nu chapter, and transferred into Phi Epsilon Omega in January 1999. During her tenure in the chapter, Soror Timeka has held several positions within the chapter. She served as the Fundraising Chairman (1999-2000), Graduate Advisor to Zeta Iota (2001-2002), Pecunious Grammateus (2001-2002), Anti-Basileus (2003-2006), and Parliamentarian (2009-2010). She has also participated on committees external to the chapter including the Chicago chapter of the National Pan-Hellenic Council, Joint Founders' Day celebration committee, the Central Region's Planning Committee for the Centennial Celebration in Washington D.C. in 2008, and was the chairman of the Central Region's Evaluations committee (2010-2014). Soror Timeka received Phi Epsilon Omega's Soror of the Year award in 2001 and Unsung Shero in 2008.

To stay current on business of the sorority and receive continuous leadership development, Soror Timeka has attended almost every Central Regional Conference and Boule since she has been in the sorority. It has been through her admirable guidance and clear vision that has helped to move our chapter forward, and has set the tone for others to follow.

While serving the sorority dutifully, Soror Timeka has shared her passion of helping others by supporting many community service organizations: MADD-Mothers Against Drunk Drivers organization, the Rainbow Coalition of Gays and Lesbians, Project Dance for Young Offenders, and Free-Hand-HIV/AIDS Impacting People.

Soror Timeka Gee has been a Probation Officer with the Cook County Social Service Department for over 15 years. She holds a Bachelor's degree in Liberal Arts from Northeastern Illinois University and a Master's Degree in Human Services Administration from Spertus College. She also has a catering business "Pink Parties Unlimited, Inc." that she manages diligently in her spare time. Additionally, she is a member of the Fellowship Missionary Baptist Church. Soror Timeka is blessed to be the mother of a son, Malachi Gee. Soror Timeka has made a positive impact on our chapter through her devout love for this precious organization and will continue to represent our chapter with the highest regards.

LaTonya Gunter
Basileus 2009-2010

Soror LaTonya Gunter is a charter member of Phi Epsilon Omega chapter. She was Sergeant-at-Arms for the Ultimate Women of Pink and Green interest group. In addition to being Basileus, she has held the offices of Philacter (1999-2002), Nominating Chairman (2004), and Epistoleus (2007-2008). During her tenure as Basileus, Soror LaTonya's goals were to keep the chapter true to its rules by making our bylaws more appropriate and conducting frequent updates and discussions on parliamentary procedure and invited Soror Deborah Underwood to conduct a parliamentary procedure workshop for the chapter. Soror LaTonya has served on the Central Region's technology committee since 2010. She also has served the chapter by being a member of the program, fundraising, bylaws, budget, nominating, membership, and social committees.

Soror LaTonya was initiated into Zeta Iota Chapter in 1990. She received her bachelor's degree in law enforcement from Western Illinois University, paralegal certificate with honors from Roosevelt University, and will receive a Master's in Business Administration with a concentration in information security in June 2014 from Keller Graduate School of

Management. She is currently working as a licensing analyst. Soror LaTonya is an extremely reliable soror and has only missed a handful of chapter meetings in the last 15 years.

Tamara McClain
Basileus 2011-2012

On the 10th day of January, 1999, Tamara McClain was humbly initiated in Nu Omicron Omega chapter of Alpha Kappa Alpha Sorority, Incorporated. From the moment that she was pinned, Soror Tamara has remained active serving Alpha Kappa Alpha Sorority, Incorporated on a local and regional level. While active in Nu Omicron Omega, Tamara served as the 67th Central Regional Conference Grammateus and Cotillion Co-Chairman. After transferring into the vibrant chapter of Phi Epsilon Omega Chapter in 2004, Tamara has served as the 2nd Anti-Basileus (2007-2008), 1st Anti-Basileus (2010-2011), Basileus (2011-2012), and Hodegos (2013-2014). She has also supported her chapter by being part of membership, social, and fundraising committees. She was Phi Epsilon Omega's Soror of the Year in 2008. She served regionally while in Phi Epsilon Omega chapter as one of the logistics chairmen for the 75th Central Regional Conference. Her commitment to her chapter sisters, the Harvey community, and leadership development affords her the ability to go beyond the call of duty in the name of Alpha Kappa Alpha.

An extremely dynamic Basileus, Soror Tamara McClain's goals for her administration included updating Phi Epsilon Omega's chapter bylaws to improve chapter operations as well as develop a practical guide that is relevant to PEO. Further, her aim was to foster and improve sisterly relations amongst chapter members as well as conduct a chapter health check to ensure compliance with all national and regional governing.

The one main element that keeps Soror Tamara constantly motivated to serve this illustrious organization in the capacity that she does is community service. Where there is a need, she attempts to provide an avenue. From the chapter's annual Back to School Rally, MLK Day Workshops, Men's/Women's Wellness presentations to the Angel Tree and Health Target Walk-a-Thons, Soror Tamara has been there to support her chapter.

Soror Tamara received her bachelor's degree in English from Western Illinois University, and master's degree in Higher Education with an emphasis in Student Development from Loyola University. She is married to her college sweetheart, and has 2 beautiful daughters. She currently works as the Multicultural Recruiting Manager at William Rainey Harper College, and also teaches Diversity as an adjunct faculty member.

Cindy N. Sanders
Basileus 2013-2014

Soror Cindy N. Sanders (Basileus 2013-2014) is a charter member of Phi Epsilon Omega chapter. She was the historian for the interest group and continued to hold that office after chartering in 1999 through 2000. She has also held the offices of Anti-Basileus (2011-2012), Standards Chairman (2005-2006), Graduate Advisor (2001-2002 & 2007-2008), and Pecunious Grammateus (2003-2004). She was also the chairman of the step-show committee for the 75th Central Regional Conference in 2009 and the co-chairman for the 80th Central Regional Conference's youth summit.

Soror Cindy has a Bachelor's degree in Elementary Education from Western Illinois University and a Master's degree in Human Services Counseling from National-Louis University. She works as a high school counselor at King College Prep where she is motivating and encouraging students to pursue their dreams and excellence. She is the proud mother of an academically and athletically talented son. She is an extremely enthusiastic person and has been one of the emcees for all of our Back to School Rallies and several other events as she exudes life and passion for all things, especially Alpha Kappa Alpha Sorority, Inc.

Soror Cindy's goals as Basileus are to continue moving the chapter forward in all areas including membership, programs, service, sisterhood, and leadership. During her tenure as Basileus, the chapter experienced great revitalization by hosting two MIPs, a wave of soror reactivations, outstanding programs, sisterly relations activities, new scholarship opportunities, increased visibility, and celebrating the chapter's fifteen years of service. Phi Epsilon Omega's total membership in 2014 has the potential to grow to 57; the largest number of active sorors since the chapter's inception. She envisioned the PEO Passport program to encourage sorors to actively participate in all dimensions of the chapter and it came to fruition with the help of her dedicated leadership team. The next chapters of Phi Epsilon Omega Chapter are still waiting to be written and Soror Cindy continues to be the chapter's cheerleader; full of energy and optimism and a leader who encourages and promotes "Service to all Mankind" because sorors know there are "Greater Laurels to Win and Greater Tasks to Begin."

PROGRAMS

The sorors of Phi Epsilon Omega chapter have "Blazed New Trails", promoted the "SPIRIT of Alpha Kappa Alpha", pursued "Economics, Sisterhood, and Partnerships", and supported "Global Leadership Through Timeless Service" in their efforts to provide numerous programs to the community. Below are examples of some of the activities in which Phi Epsilon Omega members have participated:

- Annually, the chapter hosts its Back to School Rally for the Harvey community. A signature chapter program event, the rally provides motivation as the students prepare to start their school year. Food, entertainment, book bags, school supplies, and health information is provided for students and their parents. As a part of this event in some years, a trunk party has been organized for the college bound students that have been recognized by the chapter throughout the year.
- Annually from 2004 to 2011, sorors from the chapter participated as a group in the Y-Me race for breast cancer awareness to raise funds for breast cancer research. The chapter has raised over $10,000 over the years for the Y-Me race. In October, pink lids are collected and sent along with a $100 donation for breast cancer research.
- In 2007 and 2008, chapter sorors participated in the American Diabetes Association's Walk for Diabetes and volunteered with the Chicago Diabetes Expo from 2006 to 2008.
- The chapter has participated in the Buckle Up program and has donated over 1,000 coats to the Harvey/Dixmoor community over the years on AKA Coat Day.
- Books, dictionaries, and encyclopedias were sent

to Africa in Project Send in 2001.

- Young Authors' contest was held at King elementary. A pizza party was given to the class of the winner.
- At each chapter meeting from 2004-2007, sorors donated their pocket change to the "Change Makes a Difference" program which provided a Thanksgiving dinner to a deserving family in Harvey, IL.
- 25th Supreme Tamiouchos, Soror Barbara A. McKinzie, spoke to the chapter in 2000 regarding personal investments.
- Phi Epsilon Omega chapter has held a number of Christmas programs since its inception: singing carols and playing bingo with seniors at the Harvey YMCA; providing gifts for students in classes at various Harvey schools, children with incarcerated parents, and "Toys for Tots" at Ingalls Hospital, and Christmas toy give away and party with Thornton Township in 2013
- The chapter held a Christmas dinner and celebration at Deborah's Place from 2004-2007, a not-for-profit organization that serves homeless or formerly homeless women. As a part of this celebration, sorors sang carols with the women of Deborah's Place and provided slippers, hats, and gloves as gifts. Sorors of Phi Epsilon Omega could readily see the effect the donation of goods as well as hours of fellowship made with the residents. Moreover, Deborah's Place's Director of Housing later commented the residents were quite appreciative and welcomed the Sorors of PEO to visit again. A similar activity was held for 2 years for the women at The Tabitha House in Harvey.
- Annually on the MLK Day of Service, Sorors of Phi Epsilon Omega chapter have joined forces with local community groups in Harvey and Dixmoor, Illinois to provide service to the

47

participants of the Women's Resource Assistance Program (WRAP). Chapter members provided business etiquette information, interviewing tips and resume writing advice for women seeking to reenter the workplace. Sorors also donated business suits and provided some guidelines for acceptable make-up, jewelry and attire while interviewing and working in corporate environments. Participants of the program expressed that sorors provided helpful information and were an inspiration to those women striving to reach their professional goals.

· Girls Identifying Future Targets Successfully (GIFTS) was the chapter's mentoring program with teenage girls at Rich South from 2005-2007. Each month, there was a roundtable discussion, individual outing with their mentor from the chapter, tutoring, and a group activity (laser tag, movies, plays, etc.) with sorors.

· The On Track program as well as the Ivy Reading AKAdemy was implemented at King elementary in Dixmoor, IL.

Phi Epsilon Omega chapter has participated in numerous programs with the Chicagoland Basilei Council. In 2005, the council donated $1402 to the Car Seats Save Lives program at John H. Stroger, Jr. Hospital of Cook County. This program provides car seats at a reduced rate to parents after attending a 30 minute program on child safety. Parents not able to afford the reduced rate, receive the car seat for free.

In 2006, the council endeavored to bring all the Chicagoland chapters together to participate in a joint program. As the council wanted to donate time and energy, the Chicago Diabetes Expo was a logical choice as the council would also be supporting a health target that disproportionately affects African-Americans while being able to volunteer its services in the community. The Expo was held at Navy Pier and provided education about diabetes management, prescription compliance, healthy eating and exercise to manage and prevent diabetes. Sorors staffed the registration for the 8600 people that attended. Sorors also staffed volunteer check-in, administered surveys, assisted with cooking demonstrations, and acted as ushers. Soror Daneen Edmond and Soror Tonya Weatherly participated. Prior to the event, the Basilei were provided with numerous brochures discussing diabetes and its prevention and were encouraged to discuss diabetes with their chapters. Soror Daneen Edmond, the basileus in 2006, discussed and distributed the brochures to Phi Epsilon Omega chapter and had sorors take a quiz to see if they were at risk for diabetes.

With Economics, Sisterhood, and Partnerships (ESP) and Global Leadership through Timeless Service, Phi Epsilon Omega has continued to conduct and participate in impactful programs. These international program platforms have allowed the chapter to continue ongoing programming as well as participate in and develop new initiatives.

Economics, Sisterhood, Partnerships

Sorors of Phi Epsilon Omega chapter supported the Half of the Sky Movie, sponsored by the CARE organization. Proceeds from the movie went towards the care of battered women all over the world. Lambda Tau Omega chapter was also in attendance at the movie. A group picture was taken and sent along with a message to the CARE organization describing the event and experience that was shared as a chapter.

Sorors gathered at Butler Field in 2010 for another successful Mother's Day Walk to Empower for Breast Cancer (formerly known as the Y-Me race). Team Sisters and Brothers United had 17 people participate, and raised $1,123 for the Network of Strength organization. Special thanks were extended from Soror Germayne Cade who has organized the chapter's participation in this event since 2004 for Sorors, family, and friends who supported this initiative.

In 2010, the chapter held a wellness program for 17 residents of the Harvey House (18 month residential Christian training facility that provides a recovery program for men to overcome addiction, crime, and homelessness) and the Tabitha House (a similar facility for women) to address the ESP platform of Economic Growth of the Black Family. Public Defender, Cranston Simpson, and Supervisor of the Office of the Clerk of the Circuit Court, David Will, were the guest speakers of the program. To assist these men and women in rebuilding their lives, guidelines were provided that explained the process to expunge criminal and traffic records.

On Saturday, November 20, 2010, Phi Epsilon Omega chapter partnered with Restoration Ministries of Harvey, IL, to conduct a Boxes of Love Program for the community of Harvey in time for the Thanksgiving holiday. The Boxes of Love Program included the gift of a turkey and a box of groceries for a traditional Thanksgiving dinner. Three sorors were in attendance along with other organizations in the community to feed 173 families present. To be eligible for the box of Thanksgiving dinner, each family head had to bring proof of Harvey residency in addition to showing proof of identification. Each family was given one box of love and help to their cars. Phi Epsilon Omega Chapter donated 11 turkeys, and 5 hams to Restoration Ministries for this event.

Phi Epsilon Omega Chapter conducted a Health and Wellness Program on November 7, 2010 in conjunction with our "Shades of Pink" Cotillion Committee at First Wesley Academy Church. Sorors Tamara McClain and Cindy Sanders, members of the program committee, spoke to the student participants about the importance of getting involved in a wellness program, feeling good about themselves, and being physically and mentally healthier. A hand-out about "Wellness Programs and Your Health" was given to the participants in addition to bags filled with health snacks and skin and beauty items. Cerita Smith, Health and Wellness Director at the South Side YMCA conducted a very interactive and energetic Zumba workshop. Soror Bakahia Madison conducted an interactive workshop on Mental and Physical Health Awareness for young adults. There were 7 chapter sorors and 12 students, including 6 cotillion participants and their escorts, in attendance.

The Circle of Sisterhood

On Sunday, December 19, 2010, Phi Epsilon Omega Chapter hosted a Non-Traditional Entrepreneur Program/Workshop honoring the African American women entrepreneurs that supported Phi Epsilon Omega chapter over the previous four years under the ESP Platforms. Five

African American business women were honored for their support of the following chapter initiatives: Annual fundraiser through event planning, Cotillion coordination, Ticket/Program/Calendar Design, Catering Services, and Fashion Design. These women had an opportunity to talk about how they started their businesses, and what their long term goals were for their businesses. Each person was honored with a token of appreciation and welcomed guests to a question and answer session.

Money Management and Financing your Future

On Sunday, November 21, 2010, Phi Epsilon Omega conducted a program entitled *Economic Keys to Success: Money Management and making the most of your financial future* at First Wesley Academy Church in Harvey, IL. There were 12 high school students and 3 parents in attendance at the workshop. Kimberly M. Thomas, Financial Advisor of Waddell and Reed (Chicago, IL) presented the workshop. The workshop focused on informing individuals about the financial planning process. The topics discussed in the workshop were: identifying priorities and setting financial goals, budgeting and building cash reserves, financial planning for college, monthly spending, banking and budgeting, investments opportunities, and minimizing the use of credit.

On Wednesday, December 8, 2010, Phi Epsilon Omega Chapter, along with 47 other individuals and organizations volunteered our services to pack boxes of food for the hungry families in our communities at the Greater Chicago Food Depository (GCFD) located at 4100 W. Ann Lurie Place in Chicago, Illinois. Eleven sorors were present and brought canned or boxed food to donate to the GCFD. Our volunteer efforts that evening resulted in

1,061 cases of packed food boxes weighing 33,000 pounds for 678,000 families in Cook County and beyond.

Global Leadership Through Timeless Service

Emerging Young Leaders

This signature program targeted girls in grades six through eight by providing leadership development, civic engagement, enhanced academic preparation and character building. The program was hosted initially at St. Elizabeth School 2011-2012 then at Wendell Smith School from 2012-2014. EYL Curriculum Handouts designed by Phi Epsilon Omega were given to the girls throughout the year. A graduation was also conducted for the girls to commemorate their successful completion of the program. This program has impacted over 30 girls to date.

2011 Chicagoland Emerging Young Leaders Summit

The Emerging Young Leaders Summit was a collaborative partnership among participating chapters of the Chicagoland Basilei Council. The summit brought together young ladies enrolled in various EYL programs throughout Chicagoland and Northwest Indiana areas. The day began with a nutritious breakfast followed by the excitement of First Lady Michelle Obama and Beyonce's "Let's Move" video. Sorors lead the fun and interactive activity designed to encourage healthy eating and lifestyles. The young ladies exercised and moved to the music getting them pumped and excited about the rest of the day's events. Guest speakers and talented women of Alpha Kappa Alpha Sorority, Inc. joined us in our efforts to promote the importance of Women's Health, Self-Image, Effective Use of Social Media and Traits of a Healthy Relationship. Each young lady attended three workshops where they were given the opportunity to discuss the value of self-worth, how to recognize unhealthy relationships and healthy living. The young ladies were provided a healthy lunch and a gift of an EYL journal and t-shirt to commemorate the event. The event closed with a keynote address given by Allen Bryson. Brochures and pamphlets on Women's Health, Self-Image, Effective Use of Social Media and Traits of a Healthy Relationship were distributed to the young girls.

Health

A number of chapter activites have focused on health. In 2011, a "Change for a Cure Box" was sponsored where sorors were encouraged to donate spare change and the program committee highlighted specific cancers that had high impact on the African-American Community. Sixty-three dollars was donated on behalf of Phi Epsilon Omega Chapter in honor of this partnership with the American Cancer Society.

Phi Epsilon Omega Chapter sponsored its annual Health Fair/Back to School Rally on August 14, 2011, August 12, 2012, and August 11, 2013 at the Harvey Community Center for the Harvey/Dixmoor community. The annual event was geared toward promoting health awareness and early prevention. There were 247 families registered for this event in 2011. These families had the opportunity to get a physical for school via Aunt Martha's Mobile medical unit, asthma screenings, and mental health awareness information. Food and beverages were given out to the community along with schools supplies at the end of the event. College scholarships are also awarded at the event. The Harvey Jr. Drill Team and the Kappa Leaguers from the Harvey-Markham Alumni Chapter of Kappa Alpha Psi Fraternity, Inc. performed during this event in 2011. A dance group from the RH School of the Performing Arts performed in 2013. Each year more groups from the community emerge to assist the chapter with this endeavor. In 2013, we were pleased to receive the aid of the men of Rho Zeta Lambda Chapter of Alpha Phi Alpha Fraternity, Inc., Harvey-Markham Alumni Chapter of Kappa Alpha Psi Fraternity, Inc., Omega Psi Phi Fraternity, Inc, and 40 Strong (a non-profit brotherhood that provides positive examples of finer manhood from every walk of life in the Chicago area).

Phi Epsilon Omega participates yearly in the Harvey 4th of July Parade. The chapter also advertises for the Phi Epsilon Omega Health Fair/Back to school Rally during this parade by distributing flyers and other marketing materials. Sorors march in the parade in support of the community.

Sorors were encouraged to complete a Fitness Pledge card during chapter meeting on February 3, 2012 to help promote fitness and exercise. Sorors were also instructed to trade their Pink for Red for one day only as we celebrated Pink Goes Red for a Day for heart health and wellness with the American Heart Association.

In honor of Kidney Awareness Month and American Diabetes Alert Day, the program committee passed out pamphlets and sugar-free candy to the First Wesley Academy Church Congregation and to sorors during chapter meeting on March 18, 2012.

For National Blood Pressure Awareness and American Stroke Day, the program committee highlighted these health issues which disproportionately affect the African-American community. The program included hosting a display table with information and ribbons to help bring awareness about these medical conditions to the First Wesley Academy Church congregation and to Sorors during chapter meeting on May 15, 2012.

For National Cancer Survivors Month, the chapter hosted a display table at the First Wesley Academy Church congregation and during chapter meeting and passed out ribbons and information on cancer. A Soror Survivor in our chapter was also honored.

During Breast Cancer Awareness Month, sorors were encouraged to 'Think Pink'. The program committee passed out ribbons and stickers as a tribute. The Shades of Pink Cotillion debutantes passed out pink ribbons and hosted a pink lemonade stand at First Wesley Academy Church on October 14, 2012. They collected $28.19 to help in the fight to end breast cancer.

November was Diabetes Awareness Month and information was distributed to First Wesley Academy Church Congregation and sorors during chapter meeting on November 18, 2012. A display table was set up and sugar-free candy was distributed along with pamphlets and healthy recipes.

Global Poverty

Operation Feed the Homeless has been held on Thanksgiving Day since 2011 at Corpus Christi Catholic Church in Chicago. Phi Epsilon Omega chapter volunteered to help those less fortunate by providing over 50 people with a hot meal on Thanksgiving along with members of the Haymarket Center, Nigerian Doctors Association, Coalition of Family Based Treatment, and Harvey-Markham Alumni Chapter of Kappa Alpha Psi Fraternity,

Incorporated. This experience taught those that volunteered to be thankful and have an attitude of gratitude for everything no matter how great or small.

Phi Epsilon Omega chapter partnered with Restoration Ministries to assist with their 'Boxes of Love' program. Boxes of Love provided groceries for a complete traditional Thanksgiving meal. The boxes were distributed to Harvey residents on November 19, 2011.

Chapter sorors partnered with Thornton Township to feed the community Thanksgiving Dinner on the Sunday prior to Thanksgiving in 2013. The chapter also donated 5 turkeys to families who attended this activity. Sorors served Thanksgiving dinner to the community.

For the Stamp out Hunger Campaign, Phi Epsilon Omega Chapter members volunteered at the Greater Chicago Food Depository on June 1, 2011 and November 2, 2011. Sorors helped pack boxes of food for families in need in the Chicagoland area. Proceeds from this effort went to Restoration Ministries. For this initiative, sorors also brought canned goods to chapter meeting and the items were donated to the First Wesley Academy United Methodist Church in Harvey, IL. First Wesley hosts a food pantry and a soup kitchen weekly.

Sorors assisting at the Greater Chicago Food Depository in 2011.

'PEO Goes Wild' Silent Auction was held for Heifer International during chapter meeting in May of 2011. Phi Epsilon Omega Chapter raised $250.00 and donated the proceeds to Heifer International.

The chapter hosted a Restaurant benefit night at Fuddruckers on 3/28/12 and 7/9/2013 and at Buffalo Wild Wings on 10/30/2013 and 11/1/2013. Sorors, family, and friends gathered for these evenings of fellowship and food to raise funds for Heifer International.

Economic Security

On December 3rd and 14th of 2013, chapter sorors partnered with Chicago Public School's Technical Education Department to participate in Mock Interviews and Resume Reviews for approximately 600 high schools students from 60 high schools across the state. Sorors had the opportunity to assist high school students in their quest to improve their marketability in preparation to enter the employment world.

On May 10, 2013, Phi Epsilon Omega chapter hosted an Entrepreneur Networking Seminar. Established and aspiring female minority business owners had the unique opportunity to share and receive valuable information from other entrepreneurs in the community. Attendees heard from speakers from Z'Boutique, PNC Bank, Dejanae Events, and Pink Parties Unlimited about branding, marketing, and financial planning.

Our chapter honored Black Businesses at our Illusion of a Pearl Fashion Event on June 3, 2012. The fashion show event encompassed our Economic Security Initiative where Black businesses participated in the fashion show and they were allowed to both showcase and sell their merchandise to highlight their business.

Social Justice and Human Rights

PEO took over Panera Bread in Matteson, Illinois for a Domestic Violence Remembrance project, and the theme was 'Heeling the Soul' on November 27, 2011. Women against Violence Cafe (must wear heels) Heeling the SOUL: A Community-Based agency project. Sorors donated shoes in a shoebox. Sorors in attendance created decorative boxes with inspirational statements, resources and pictures. The shoe boxes symbolize hope and resiliency for domestic violence survivors. The shoes were donated to the Haymarket Center.

Phi Epsilon Omega utilized the Angel Tree Network to benefit children with incarcerated parents. Sorors helped spread Christmas Joy in the 2011 holiday season by adopting a child with incarcerated parents and providing them with gifts for Christmas.

In 2012, Phi Epsilon Omega again participated in Angel Tree Project by donating gifts to the students at Wendell Phillips School. Several students have incarcerated parents and live below the poverty line.

Stop the Violence Rally and Voters Registration Drive was held on September 22, 2012. The program was hosted by Harvey Markham Alumni Chapter of Kappa Alpha Psi Fraternity. Cease Fire, Delta Sigma Theta and First Wesley United Methodist Church also participated in the event. Fifteen voters were registered and over 50 people were in attendance during the event.

The program committee hosted 'PEO Cares: Toiletry Drive 2012' during the months of October-December. Sorors compiled collected items into care packages, which were donated to Crisis Center for South Suburbia benefitting victims of domestic violence

International Leadership Training

In 2012, Phi Epsilon Omega held a membership training workshop at its annual June chapter retreat. Soror Pamela Bates Porch, the Central Region representative to the International Membership committee, was the featured guest speaker. Her powerful message resonated with chapter sorors and was an appropriate segue into the officers' training workshop, conducted by the Standards Chairman.

Chapter sorors with Soror Pamela Bates Porch, Central Region Representative to the International Membership Committee

The Founders' Bucks initiative of 2013 rewarded sorors for attending chapter activities like chapter meeting, fundraising events, and program activities. Sorors earned bucks for their attendance as well as successfully answering chapter trivia questions. Quarterly, sorors were able to "shop" at the Founders' Bucks table where they could purchase items with their Founders' Bucks.

The PEO Pearl Passport initiative was developed in 2013 to encourage sorors to actively participate in various chapter activities throughout the year. Sorors earned stamps throughout the year for attending chapter meetings, programs, fundraisers, and other activities. A raffle for prizes was held at the December 2013 chapter meeting rewarding active participation.

Professional Public Speaker Soror Germayne Cade facilitated a motivational workshop to chapter sorors during our Chapter Retreat on June 8, 2013. She spoke about how to make great choices, looking for the positive in every situation, and being the best you can be moving forward.

Environmental Stewardship and Sustainability

In celebration of National Arbor Day, the program committee planted a tree on May 20, 2012 in honor of our chapter in the Harvey Community. The tree planting was featured on the Harvey Community City Marquee.

The chapter also adopted a lot from the city of Harvey in 2013. During the 2013 Membership Intake Process, the candidates (now sorors) chose the lot as their community service project (entitled 'Think Pink, Live Green, Love the Lot') and decorated the lot in September 2013. Sorors attend to the lot every month and inform the city when the grass needs to be cut.

SOCIAL

To foster sisterhood, the chapter has hosted numerous activities each year to promote sisterly relations. Each year, sorors look forward to the soror brunch, book clubs, and Christmas party. The chapter anniversary celebration, AKA Game Night, strolling parties, summer picnics, slumber parties, "A Taste of AKA" potluck dinners, AKAerobics, ice cream socials, and soror tea are examples of other events scheduled throughout the years to promote our sisterly relations. During the annual chapter retreat in June, various activities have been held to strengthen the bonds of sisterhood.

Although chapter meeting is a business meeting, sorors host chapter meeting each month and provide food. This has allowed sorors time to fellowship before and after the meeting. Chapter meetings have been held at the Harvey Public Library, Harvey YMCA, Grand Prairie Library, IIT (Perlstein Hall), Julian High School, First Wesley Academy United Methodist Church, and the Harvey Community Center.

Sorors have enjoyed participating in the welcome reception at the Central Regional Conference since 2004. Sorors have used this as an opportunity to bond during practices while creating and learning a stroll for the reception. In 2004, sorors wore pink and green shawls crocheted by DoubleStitch, a company owned by Phi Epsilon Omega Soror Erika Simmons and her twin, Monika Simmons.

Soror Timeka Gee wearing DoubleStitch crocheted shawl

The first anniversary of the chartering of Phi Epsilon Omega chapter was celebrated with a dinner and brief program with unique awards at the Beverly Woods Restaurant and Banquet Hall in Chicago, Illinois. Chapter sorors ate, fellowshipped, and sang the chapter song to commemorate the occasion.

The 5th anniversary week included 'A Pink Champagne Celebration' a party open to the public held at Kompel on January 17, 2004. Chapter sorors wore pink. A midnight brunch was held for sorors only before Joint Founders' Day in Oakbrook, IL on January 23, 2004.

Sorors at 5th anniversary celebration.

Sorors with 26th Central Regional Director Soror Dorothy Buckhanan Wilson at midnight brunch.

A week of activities was held to celebrate the chapter's 10th anniversary. The first event was a brunch held at 94 West Steak and Seafood Restaurant. Soror Nadine C. Bonds, the chapter's chartering Central Regional Director, was in attendance as a surprise guest speaker. Numerous awards, gifts, and certificates were given to sorors in appreciation for their service throughout the years. A book club and wine sip was hosted by Soror Tanya Foucher-Weekley at her home. A 'Passion Pink Pamper Party' was held at Sensual Steps Salon. Sorors were able to purchase shoes and receive spa services. The week culminated with a party held at Frankie Z's in Chicago on January 23, 2009. Chapter sorors wore black with pink pearls and partied the night away. Numerous family and friends came to help the chapter celebrate.

Sorors and friends at 10th anniversary celebration

The 15th anniversary celebration has been scheduled to occur on January 23-25, 2014 with an anniversary toast at L26 on January 23rd, PEO Soror Roundup on January 24th, and 15th Anniversary Rededication Ceremony and Banquet at the Smart Museum of Art on January 25th.

A few sorors from Phi Epsilon Omega were able to attend the Centennial Founders' Day Celebration in Washington DC. Phi Epsilon Omega sorors that stayed in Chicago hosted a Centennial Founders' Day celebration at Seven Ten Lanes on January 15, 2008. Sorors from numerous Chicago chapters attended.

Sorors in Washington DC for Centennial Founders' Day Celebration

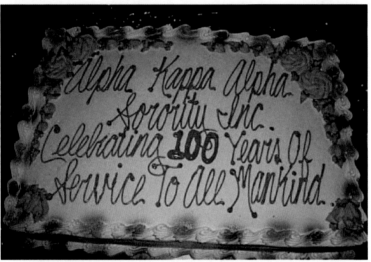

Sorors in Chicago for Centennial Founders' Day Celebration

Sorors from Phi Epsilon Omega chapter participated in the Symbolic Centennial Walk of 1908 steps that occurred at the same time around the world on June 28, 2008. In Chicago, Phi Epsilon Omega and 9 other Chicagoland chapters began and ended their 1908 steps at the Theta Omega Community Service Center.

Sorors at Symbolic Centennial Walk at Theta Omega Community Service Center

Sorors traveled to Washington DC for the Centennial Boule. Celebrations were held on the airplane on the way to DC, at the airport, in the plenary sessions, at Howard University, and at restaurants and hotels all around the city.

Sorors with 26th Supreme Basileus Soror Linda M. White at airport in DC

Sorors at Centennial Boule in DC with 27th Supreme Grammateus Soror
Dorothy Buckhanan Wilson

Sorors at Centennial Boule in DC with 27th Supreme Basileus Soror Barbara A. McKinzie

72

FUNDRAISERS AND SCHOLARSHIP

Fundraisers have included Candlelight Bowling, fashion events, restaurant benefit nights, ETA Theater Night, P.R.O.M. Night, a Chicago Bulls' game, a midnight cruise, and Sippin' Around the World (a wine tasting event). In 2003 and 2004, the chapter sponsored the Illinois Drill Team Association's (IDTA) Competition. With no funds from the chapter and 12 hours of volunteer time at the IDTA's competition, thousands of dollars were secured for the chapter to provide scholarships and donations to health targets.

P.R.O.M. Night Awards Gala (Promote, Reward Outstanding Milestones for Today's Youth) was held in 2003 and 2004 to recognize youth for their achievement in Community Service, Arts, Science, Math and students living with sickle cell anemia (2003) and diabetes (2004). Scholarships were also given to students for the Presidential Freedom Scholarship and the P.E.A.R.L. Scholarship (Providing Education Assistance to Reward Levels of achievement). The venue for the P.R.O.M. Night Awards Gala was the Flossmoor Country Club where sorors, friends, family, students from Rich South High School and other guests were able to 'relive' or experience Prom night.

Sorors at P.R.O.M. Night in 2004

Sippin' Around the World featured wines and foods from various countries or states and was held annually from 2007 to 2010. It was held at the Joffrey Ballet studios in 2007 and 2008, at Mars Gallery in 2009, and in 2010 was held at the Alpha Phi Alpha Community Center.

Starting in 2007, the chapter has sponsored the annual Shades of Pink Cotillion. Dances for all of the cotillions except the 2013 cotillion were choreographed by Soror Ceshia Wilder and her husband for the debutantes and escorts. Chapter sorors volunteered their time to teach about etiquette, health, and other topics. The debutantes also completed community service hours and sold ads and tickets. The proceeds have all been given back to the debutantes as scholarships and awards. In 2013, there were 5 debutantes and over $7,000 in scholarships and awards was given to the young ladies. Each escort received a $50 visa gift card.

Debutantes and escorts at 2008 Shades of Pink Cotillion

Each year, the chapter has selected a health target to donate part of the proceeds of fundraisers. Phi Epsilon Omega chapter has supported the foundations for Sickle Cell Disease (1999 and 2003), Systemic Lupus Erythematosus (2000), Sarcoidosis (2001), Multiple Sclerosis (2002), Diabetes Mellitus (2004), Childhood Obesity (2005), Allergy, Asthma, March of Dimes (2010), American Cancer Society (2011), and more. The remainder of the proceeds of fundraisers is given as scholarships.

Soror Bakahia Madison presenting check to representative from the Life with Lupus Guild

The chapter also used benefit nights at restaurants (Fuddruckers and Buffalo Wild Wings) to provide additional funds for Heifer International, one of the international program initiatives (global poverty) for Global Leadership Through Timeless Service.

Fundraiser chairman Hareder McDowell and her committee added 'AKA and a Movie' to Phi Epsilon Omega's repertoire of fundraisers in 2013. Sorors and their friends viewed *Temptation: Confessions of a Marriage Counselor* at the Showplace Icon Theater in Chicago, IL and *Best Man Holiday* at Hollywood Boulevard in Woodridge, IL. These events raised over $1,000 for scholarships.

In 2001, the chapter voted to name the scholarships that it had been awarding as the P.E.A.R.L. Scholarship (Providing Education Assistance to Reward Levels of achievement). The chapter has given this scholarship out annually since 2001 to high school seniors. From 2002 to 2006, the chapter also awarded the Presidential Freedom Scholarship, a scholarship matched by the sorority through a grant, to deserving high school seniors.

One of the goals of Soror Daneen Edmond while she was basileus was to start a chapter foundation. A committee was established but the goal was not accomplished before the end of her administration in 2006. In 2011, Soror Daneen researched starting an EAF chapter endowment fund. She brought the information to the chapter and solicited enough funds to initiate an endowed fund entitled the Phi Epsilon Omega P.E.A.R.L. scholarship fund. Once capitalized at $20,000, the chapter will be able to provide additional scholarships to students from the fund.

On January 29, 2013, the chapter was devastated when the 15 year old daughter of one its first initiates was shot and killed after school by gang members shooting recklessly into a crowd of students. Hadiya Pendleton was an honor student and a majorette at Dr. Martin Luther King, Jr. College Preparatory High School who just returned home from performing at the inauguration of President Barack Obama. To honor Soror Cleopatra Cowley-Pendleton's daughter, the chapter gave a scholarship in her name to a college-bound graduate of King College Prep in the fall of 2013.

TIMELESS HISTORICAL PERSPECTIVES OF

PHI EPSILON OMEGA

Phi Epsilon Omega Chapter

Harvey, Illinois

2011 Oral History Transcripts

Date: September 9, 2011

Soror Sandra Rush-Atkins' interview by Soror Germayne Cade –
Chapter Historian

Interview Questions

1. Soror Germayne Cade asked: Why did you decide to become a
member of AKA?

Soror Sandra Rush replied: *I was the first member of my family to go
away to college. So, Alpha Kappa Alpha Sorority Inc., through its
service projects and fundraising events, had a high level of visibility on
campus. Based on what I observed, I set a goal to join Alpha Kappa
Alpha Sorority Inc. as a way of fulfilling personal goals to help my
local community and abroad.*

2. Soror Germayne Cade asked: **Why did you decide to join or start PEO?**

Soror Sandra Rush replied: *Soror Daneen Edmond, who is a chartering member of PEO, invited me to join the chapter based upon my character and ability to work well with others. I graciously accepted the invitation. As I reflect on the past few years, I know that PEO is a great fit for me. I will continue to help the chapter achieve its goals and prosper.*

3. Soror Germayne Cade asked: **What are your proudest moments of being an AKA?**

Soror Sandra Rush replied: *My proudest moments are becoming a member of Alpha Kappa Alpha Sorority Inc., servicing the community year after year, and being voted 2010 Soror of the Year.*

4. Soror Germayne Cade asked: Conversely, what are disappointment moments...or regrets, if any?

Soror Sandra Rush replied: No regrets.

5. Soror Germayne Cade asked: **What are your thoughts on the direction of PEO?**

Soror Sandra Rush replied: PEO is headed in a positive direction. As we work together on the various National Program initiatives, we are more focused on what has to be done to move PEO forward. Our sisterly activities help keep us connected.

6. Soror Germayne Cade asked: **What will she need to accomplish to be a truly great chapter?**

Soror Sandra Rush replied: In order to be a truly great chapter, we will have to continue to be sisterly and work diligently as a chapter to achieve and exceed all goals that have been set by the Supreme Basileus.

7. Soror Germayne Cade asked: **Can you see the growth of PEO from inception until present?**

Soror Sandra Rush replied: I joined PEO in December of 2007. Over the past 4 years, I have definitely seen some positive trends as sorors remain active year after year and commit themselves to the work that has to be done in the spirit of AKA. I really like the level of commitment from the chartering members and how they are always willing to share pertinent information to help those of us who are fairly new to the chapter.

8. Soror Germayne Cade asked: **What is your vision for PEO at 50 years (2049)?**

Soror Sandra Rush replied: My vision is to help PEO strive to become one of the most recognized chapters in the Central Region. We will continue to work to win awards and get recognition at the Regional & Leadership Conferences as well as the Boule for years to come.

Phi Epsilon Omega Chapter

Harvey, Illinois

2011 Oral History Transcripts

Date: April 30, 2011

Soror Michelle Rainey's interview by Soror Germayne Cade – Chapter Historian

1. Soror Germayne Cade asked: **Why did you decide to become a member of AKA**

Soror Michelle Rainey replied: *I became a member of AKA because I was impressed with what members did in the community and the members that I knew always appeared poised and confident. I wanted to be part of a group of women such as those members of AKA.*

2. Soror Germayne Cade asked: **Why did you decide to join or start PEO?**

Soror Michelle Rainey replied: *I decided to join PEO because a few of my good friends were members of the chapter. Also after spending time with the chapter members and experiencing all that they did for the Harvey community I knew that this was the chapter for me.*

3. Soror Germayne Cade asked: **What are your proudest moments of being an AKA?**

Soror Michelle Rainey replied: *My proudest moments of being an AKA are being able to help the community and the bonds that I have established with my chapter members.*

4. Soror Germayne Cade asked: Conversely, what are disappointment moments...or regrets, if any?

Soror Michelle Rainey replied: *No regrets.*

5. Soror Germayne Cade asked: **What are your thoughts on the direction of PEO?**

Soror Michelle Rainey replied: *I would like for PEO to do more in the community and develop an "annual" signature fundraising event.*

6. Soror Germayne Cade asked: **What will she need to accomplish to be a truly great chapter?**

Soror Michelle Rainey replied: *Obtain a better knowledge of protocol and develop a better sense of tolerance and diversity in dealing with chapter members. Also to recognize and nurture individual strengths while gently acknowledging weaknesses.*

7. Soror Germayne Cade asked: Can you see the growth of PEO from inception until present?

Soror Michelle Rainey replied: *I was not a member at the time of inception. However, I have seen growth in my 5 years as a member.*

8. Soror Germayne Cade asked: What is your vision for PEO at 50 years (2049)?

Soror Michelle Rainey replied: *I envision PEO being a staple in the Harvey community as well as well known for its service in the Sorority.*

Phi Epsilon Omega Chapter

Harvey, Illinois

2011 Oral History Transcripts

Date: October 15, 2011

Soror Cindy N. Sanders' interview by Soror Germayne Cade – Chapter Historian

1. Soror Germayne Cade asked: Why did you decide to become a member of AKA

Soror Cindy Sanders replied: *I had participated in the Miss Fashionetta Cotillion and I received two scholarships and I was in love with everything that the Sorority believed in and I wanted to be a part so I could do those same things that sorors did for me back then.*

2. Soror Germayne Cade asked: **Why did you decide to join or start PEO?**

Soror Cindy Sanders replied: *We wanted to start a revolution of Alpha Kappa Alpha Service, Commitment and Scholarship to the Harvey Community. We were already friends so the next logical step was for us to combine our talents and resources to form our chapter and the rest is history.*

3. Soror Germayne Cade asked: **What are your proudest moments of being an AKA?**

Soror Cindy Sanders replied: *There are so many high points but my proudest moment is right now. I am very proud to serve as the Anti-Basileus of Phi Epsilon Omega.*

4. Soror Germayne Cade asked: Conversely, what are disappointment moments...or regrets, if any?

Soror Cindy Sanders replied: *None*

5. Soror Germayne Cade asked: **What are your thoughts on the direction of PEO?**

Soror Cindy Sanders replied: *We are on an upward spiral and our destiny is bright. We must pull together because teamwork makes the dream work and there are "Greater Laurels to Win and Greater Task to Begin" We must continue to be a vehicle of service for the Harvey Community and Globally. Service is our Signature.*

6. Soror Germayne Cade asked: **What will she need to accomplish to be a truly great chapter?**

Soror Cindy Sanders replied: *She will need to have members who are focused on preserving her history and members who continually add value to the causes that she champions.*

7. Soror Germayne Cade asked: **Can you see the growth of PEO from inception until present?**

Soror Cindy Sanders replied: *I am proud of what our chapter has accomplished in the past 11 years however we have much to do in service to mankind. We must continue to challenge ourselves via exemplary programs, et al.*

8. Soror Germayne Cade asked: **What is your vision for PEO at 50 years (2049)?**

Soror Cindy Sanders replied: *I look forward to celebrating our Golden Anniversary. I will be 76 years young. PEO will be a chapter that represents our Founders' goals and ideals while paying tribute to the Charter Member's uniqueness. We would have Blazed New Trails, had ESP, provided Global Leadership with Timeless Service, loved Soror Dorothy and much, much more. I am truly excited about the chapters in the Phi Epsilon Omega storybook. I feel that she will surpass all our expectations and take her place as a prominent member of Central Region*

Phi Epsilon Omega Chapter

Harvey, Illinois

2011 Oral History Transcripts

Date: June 11, 2011

Soror Tamara McClain's interview by Soror Germayne Cade – Chapter Historian

1. Soror Germayne Cade asked: **Why did you decide to become a member of AKA**

Soror Tamara McClain replied: *I wanted to become a member of Alpha Kappa Alpha Sorority, Incorporated in college and saw that the prestige in the women wearing pink and green on campus. These were educated women who were the smartest on campus and dressed meticulously. Once I found out the type of service that these young women were doing after college in the community, the type of careers they held and the fact that they all doing this while doing multiple tasks in their life, I knew that I wanted to belong to a group of women that gave back to the community and loved doing the service in a in positive way. I also researched the rich legacy that the women of Alpha Kappa Alpha had from post slavery, through the civil rights era to the present. Who wouldn't want to be part of this rich tradition of sisterhood?*

2. Soror Germayne Cade asked: Why did you decide to join or start PEO?

Soror Tamara McClain replied: *I decided to transfer into Phi Epsilon Omega Chapter because I wanted to work, and bond with a small chapter of young Back women who had the same interests, family structures, and goals as I did. I have known some of them since I was in college and had forged friendships with these women over the years outside of the sorority. But, it is these friendships that have helped to sustain the structure of the chapter in the years that I have been affiliated with.*

3. Soror Germayne Cade asked: What are your proudest moments of being an AKA?

Soror Tamara McClain replied: *My proudest moment of being a woman of Alpha Kappa Alpha is when I was sworn in as the Basileus of this Chapter. I have had the best mentors and beloved sisters that have guided me in this direction of leadership, and have instilled great values and expectations that will equip me the vision and determination to lead this chapter to the next level of success in the Central Region. I owe this moment to my chartering members as my guiding spirits of greatness.*

4. Soror Germayne Cade asked: Conversely, what are disappointment moments...or regrets, if any?

Soror Tamara McClain replied: *I have no regrets at all in terms of my decisions of becoming a member of this organization. However I*

85

do regret how the situation with our former 28th Supreme Basileus Soror Barbara McKinzie was handled in the media and internally within the organization.

5. Soror Germayne Cade asked: **What are your thoughts on the direction of PEO?**

Soror Tamara McClain replied: *I believe that our chartering members set a course of great leadership in 1999, and have passed that torch of leadership to many Sorors over the years that will allow Phi Epsilon Omega chapter to leave a legacy of commitment of service to the community of Harvey/Dixmoor and beyond. We have visionaries in this chapter, and with educated women with visions, great things can be accomplished. I know that as our chapter continues to grow, we will be able to accomplish many goals not only set by the chapter, but also through the international platforms. Phi Epsilon Omega Chapter will receive some regional awards, and will have members to serve on the regional and national level of this organization.*

6. Soror Germayne Cade asked: **What will she need to accomplish to be a truly great chapter?**

Soror Tamara McClain replied: *Phi Epsilon Omega is already a great chapter. The question is, when and how can she be greater? In my mind, we should always strive to be better than we were yesterday. We are constantly striving to be better leaders in the roles that we take on every two years, and become more versed with Alpha Kappa Alpha Sorority knowledge. The more that we know, the better and wiser we can and will be. Once we have achieved the set goals on all levels of Alpha Kappa Alpha Sorority, Incorporated, that is what will make us a great chapter.*

7. Soror Germayne Cade asked: **Can you see the growth of PEO from inception until present?**

Soror Tamara McClain replied: *The growth that I see from 1999 until now is socially, mentally and spiritually. Socially, we are more involved and committed to communities outside of Harvey/Dixmoor. We have partnered with several organizations,*

Greek and non-Greek lettered organizations in order to execute the international program platforms and health targets. We have grown mentally within this organization by gaining a plethora of knowledge about this organization and how it helps to feed and stimulate our minds to serve in the mannerism and mindset of our founders. Lastly, we have grown spiritually in the name of sisterhood to carry out the mission of this "sisterhood" holistically. You have to really love your sisters in this sisterhood the way we do to carry on the legacy of our founders in the spirit of Alpha Kappa Alpha Sorority, Incorporated. We live in these roles every day, and it we love the bond she has afforded us.

8. Soror Germayne Cade asked: **What is your vision for PEO at 50 years (2049)?**

Soror Tamara McClain replied: *My vision for Phi Epsilon Omega Chapter is to have a foundation created in honor of our annual fundraiser that can provide an outlet for young Black Women. I envision us to remain small, but have larger ambitious goals and results.*

REGIONAL CONTRIBUTIONS AND AWARDS

Since its inception in 1999, Phi Epsilon Omega has been active not only on the chapter level but on the regional level in its pursuit of excellence and for service to all mankind.

Soror Bakahia Madison was the co-chair for the 2003 Joint Founders' Day Celebration and chair for the 2004 Joint Founders' Day Celebration. She also served on the steering committee for the 68th Central Regional Conference as Workshops Chairman in 2002 (Soror Tanya Foucher-Weekley was the co-chair) and on the Central Region's Technology committee from 2006-2010. Soror Madison served as one of the General Conference Chairmen when the chapter hosted the 75th Central Regional Conference along with Phi Kappa Omega in Schaumburg, IL in 2009. Several other sorors from the chapter chaired conference committees in 2009: Sorors Daneen Edmond and Tamara McClain chaired the Logistics committee, Soror Tanya Foucher-Weekley chaired the Budget and Finance committee, Soror Toya Campbell chaired the VIP/Courtesies committee and Soror Sandra Rush-Atkins was the co-chairman, Soror Cindy N. Sanders chaired the Step-show committee, and Soror Tonya Weatherly chaired the Welcome Reception committee.

For the 2014 Central Regional Conference, Soror Tamara McClain chaired the workshops committee with Soror Shawanda Jennings as co-chair and Soror Tonya Weatherly chaired the welcome reception committee with Soror Hareder McDowell as the co-chair. Soror Bakahia

Madison was the chairman (Soror Cindy N. Sanders, co-chairman) of the youth summit held off-site at King College Prep High School located at 4445 S. Drexel in Chicago, IL. The school was chosen as it was attended by the late Hadiya Pendleton, daughter of Soror Cleopatra Cowley-Pendleton.

Phi Epsilon Omega Chapter was the Philacters committee for the 2000 Central Regional Conference (with Soror Bakahia Madison as Chairman) and assisted Phi Kappa Omega chapter as the Philacters committee for the 2001 Central Regional Conference. The chapter won an award for the most sorors attending Central Regional Conference for a small chapter in 2001. Due to the diligence of membership chair, Soror Charlesnika Evans, the chapter reached Pearl level for membership in 2004.

Soror Daneen Edmond was voted Outstanding Basileus for the Central Region at the 72nd Central Regional Conference. Soror Edmond was also a Central Region Heritage Committee member from 2006-2010 and assisted with evaluations for chapters in the Great Lakes Region and chapter re-evaluations in the Central Region. Soror Timeka Gee served on the Central Region's Centennial Celebration planning committee in 2008 and as the chairman for the Central Region's Evaluations committee from 2010-2014. Soror LaTonya Gunter served on the Central Region's Technology – Chapter Website Compliance committee from 2010 - 2014.

Phi Epsilon Omega chapter has boasted a diverse membership with sorors in a broad spectrum of occupations. The chapter has consisted of teachers, counselors, therapists, accountants, lawyers, nurses, doctors, bankers, realtors, fashion designers, consultants, and numerous other fields of employment and expertise. Due to this, Phi Epsilon Omega chapter sorors know they can succeed in implementing the programs of the sorority and look forward to serving the local community, the region, and the sorority for many years to come.

BIBLIOGRAPHY

McDowell, Hareder. "Phi Epsilon Omega Hosts Shades of Pink Scholarship Cotillion." Ivy Leaf 90, no.2 (Summer 2011): 30.

Evans, Charlesnika. "Phi Epsilon Omega Hosts Annual Sippin' Around the World Fundraiser." Ivy Leaf 89, no.3 (Fall 2010): 65.

Evans, Charlesnika. "Phi Epsilon Omega Hosts Wellness Program." Ivy Leaf 89, no.1 (Spring 2010): 68.

Evans, Charlesnika. "Phi Epsilon Omega Celebrates 10th Anniversary." Ivy Leaf 88, no. 2 (Summer 2009): 79.

"Centennial Anniversary Honor Roll." Ivy Leaf 86, no. 2 (Summer 2007): 25.

"Phi Epsilon Omega Presents 2007 P.E.A.R.L. Scholarship Cotillion." Ivy Leaf 86, no.2 (Summer 2007): 54.

Edmond, Daneen. "Phi Epsilon Omega Hosts 6th Annual Back to School Rally." Ivy Leaf 85, no. 4 (Winter 2006): 88.

Wilson, Nikki Laury. "Phi Epsilon Omega Walks for Health." Ivy Leaf 85, no. 4 (Winter 2006): 88.

"Chicagoland Basilei Council Donates to Car Seat Safety Program." Ivy Leaf 85, no.1 (Spring 2006): 76-77.

"Membership Making A Difference: 2006 Reclamation and Retention Initiative Recognitions." Ivy Leaf 85, no.1 (Spring 2006): 34

"Phi Epsilon Omega Reaches Out to Harvey-Dixmoor Community." Ivy Leaf 83, no. 2 (Summer 2004): 73

Zancan, Darren. "'Shades of Pink' 2007 Cotillion." NWI Times News (Munster), March 28, 2007.

Alpha Kappa Alpha Sorority, Inc. 72nd Central Regional Conference Agenda, April 12-15, 2006, Reactivated Sorors, page 33

Alpha Kappa Alpha Sorority, Inc. 73rd Central Regional Conference Agenda, May 24-27, 2007, Reactivated Sorors, page 43

Alpha Kappa Alpha Sorority, Inc. 75th Central Regional Conference Agenda, April 16-19, 2009, Reactivated Sorors, page 45

Alpha Kappa Alpha Sorority, Inc. Regional Director's Report, 71st Central Regional Conference, April 7-10, 2005, Pearl Level Chapters, page 3

Alpha Kappa Alpha Sorority, Inc. 71st Central Regional Conference Agenda, April 7-10, 2005, Graduate Chapter Sorors of the Year, page 27

Alpha Kappa Alpha Sorority, Inc. 72nd Central Regional Conference Agenda, April 12-15, 2006, Graduate Chapter Sorors of the Year, page 27

Alpha Kappa Alpha Sorority, Inc. 72nd Central Regional Conference Agenda, April 12-15, 2006, Conference Committees, Awards, page 33

Alpha Kappa Alpha Sorority, Inc. 73rd Central Regional Conference Agenda, May 24-27, 2007, 2007 Chapter Sorors of the Year, page 40

Alpha Kappa Alpha Sorority, Inc. 73rd Central Regional Conference Agenda, May 24-27, 2007, Committees, Regional Centennial Planning Committee (erroneously listed as Boule Luncheon), page 47

Alpha Kappa Alpha Sorority, Inc. 74th Central Regional Conference Agenda, April 10-13, 2008, 2008 Chapter Sorors of the Year, page 47

Alpha Kappa Alpha Sorority, Inc. 75th Central Regional Conference Agenda, April 16-19, 2009, 2009 Chapter Sorors of the Year, page 43

Alpha Kappa Alpha Sorority, Inc. 76th Central Regional Conference Agenda, March 25-28, 2010, 2010 Chapter Sorors of the Year, page 37

Alpha Kappa Alpha Sorority, Inc. 78th Central Regional Conference Agenda, April 26-29, 2012, 2012 Chapter Sorors of the Year, page 43 and 81

Alpha Kappa Alpha Sorority, Inc. 68th Central Regional Conference Program, April 11-14, 2002, Conference Steering Committee

Alpha Kappa Alpha Sorority, Inc. 75th Central Regional Conference Special Guest Guide, April 2009, Protocol Committee members

LeCompte, Peggy Lewis, Alpha Kappa Alpha Sorority, Inc. Centennial Boule Report, July 11-18, 2008, Report of the Central Regional Heritage Committee, page 84

Alpha Kappa Alpha Sorority, Inc. April 12-15, 2006, *Meeting of the 72nd Central Regional Conference*, Conference Awards Summary, Outstanding Basileus – Yvonne Perkins Award

Alpha Kappa Alpha Sorority, Inc., Phi Epsilon Omega Chapter
March 19, 1999, *Meeting of Alpha Kappa Alpha Sorority, Inc.,
Phi Epsilon Omega Chapter.*

Alpha Kappa Alpha Sorority, Inc., Phi Epsilon Omega Chapter.
October 17, 1999, *Meeting of Alpha Kappa Alpha Sorority, Inc.,
Phi Epsilon Omega Chapter.*

Alpha Kappa Alpha Sorority, Inc., Phi Epsilon Omega Chapter.
November 21, 1999, *Meeting of Alpha Kappa Alpha Sorority,
Inc., Phi Epsilon Omega Chapter.*

Alpha Kappa Alpha Sorority, Inc., Phi Epsilon Omega Chapter.
February 20, 2000, *Meeting of Alpha Kappa Alpha Sorority, Inc.,
Phi Epsilon Omega Chapter.*

Alpha Kappa Alpha Sorority, Inc., Phi Epsilon Omega Chapter.
March 21, 2000. *Meeting of Alpha Kappa Alpha Sorority, Inc.,
Phi Epsilon Omega Chapter.*

Alpha Kappa Alpha Sorority, Inc., Phi Epsilon Omega Chapter.
September 17, 2000. *Meeting of Alpha Kappa Alpha Sorority,
Inc., Phi Epsilon Omega Chapter.*

Alpha Kappa Alpha Sorority, Inc., Phi Epsilon Omega Chapter.
October 19, 2000, *Meeting of Alpha Kappa Alpha Sorority, Inc.,
Phi Epsilon Omega Chapter.*

Alpha Kappa Alpha Sorority, Inc., Phi Epsilon Omega Chapter.
November 19, 2000. *Meeting of Alpha Kappa Alpha Sorority,
Inc., Phi Epsilon Omega Chapter.*

Alpha Kappa Alpha Sorority, Inc., Phi Epsilon Omega Chapter.
January 21, 2001, *Meeting of Alpha Kappa Alpha Sorority, Inc.,
Phi Epsilon Omega Chapter.*

Alpha Kappa Alpha Sorority, Inc., Phi Epsilon Omega Chapter. April 29, 2001, *Meeting of Alpha Kappa Alpha Sorority, Inc., Phi Epsilon Omega Chapter.*

Alpha Kappa Alpha Sorority, Inc., Phi Epsilon Omega Chapter. April 21, 2002, *Meeting of Alpha Kappa Alpha Sorority, Inc., Phi Epsilon Omega Chapter.*

Alpha Kappa Alpha Sorority, Inc., Phi Epsilon Omega Chapter. November 17, 2002, *Meeting of Alpha Kappa Alpha Sorority, Inc., Phi Epsilon Omega Chapter.*

Alpha Kappa Alpha Sorority, Inc., Phi Epsilon Omega Chapter. February 16, 2003, *Meeting of Alpha Kappa Alpha Sorority, Inc., Phi Epsilon Omega Chapter.*

Alpha Kappa Alpha Sorority, Inc., Phi Epsilon Omega Chapter. December 21, 2003, *Meeting of Alpha Kappa Alpha Sorority, Inc., Phi Epsilon Omega Chapter.*

Alpha Kappa Alpha Sorority, Inc., Phi Epsilon Omega Chapter. March 21, 2004, *Meeting of Alpha Kappa Alpha Sorority, Inc., Phi Epsilon Omega Chapter.*

Alpha Kappa Alpha Sorority, Inc., Phi Epsilon Omega Chapter. December 19, 2004, *Meeting of Alpha Kappa Alpha Sorority, Inc., Phi Epsilon Omega Chapter.*

Alpha Kappa Alpha Sorority, Inc., Phi Epsilon Omega Chapter. May 15, 2005, *Meeting of Alpha Kappa Alpha Sorority, Inc., Phi Epsilon Omega Chapter.*

Alpha Kappa Alpha Sorority, Inc., Phi Epsilon Omega Chapter. September 18, 2005, *Meeting of Alpha Kappa Alpha Sorority, Inc., Phi Epsilon Omega Chapter.*

Alpha Kappa Alpha Sorority, Inc., Phi Epsilon Omega Chapter. May 21, 2006, *Meeting of Alpha Kappa Alpha Sorority, Inc., Phi Epsilon Omega Chapter.*

Alpha Kappa Alpha Sorority, Inc., Phi Epsilon Omega Chapter. April 20, 2008, *Meeting of Alpha Kappa Alpha Sorority, Inc., Phi Epsilon Omega Chapter.*

Alpha Kappa Alpha Sorority, Inc., Phi Epsilon Omega Chapter. September 28, 2008, *Meeting of Alpha Kappa Alpha Sorority, Inc., Phi Epsilon Omega Chapter.*

Alpha Kappa Alpha Sorority, Inc., Phi Epsilon Omega Chapter. November 15, 2009, *Meeting of Alpha Kappa Alpha Sorority, Inc., Phi Epsilon Omega Chapter.*

Alpha Kappa Alpha Sorority, Inc., Phi Epsilon Omega Chapter. November 21, 2010, *Meeting of Alpha Kappa Alpha Sorority, Inc., Phi Epsilon Omega Chapter.*

Alpha Kappa Alpha Sorority, Inc., Phi Epsilon Omega Chapter. April 17, 2011, *Meeting of Alpha Kappa Alpha Sorority, Inc., Phi Epsilon Omega Chapter.*

Alpha Kappa Alpha Sorority, Inc., Phi Epsilon Omega Chapter. November 20, 2011, *Meeting of Alpha Kappa Alpha Sorority, Inc., Phi Epsilon Omega Chapter.*

Alpha Kappa Alpha Sorority, Inc., Phi Epsilon Omega Chapter. May 20, 2012, *Meeting of Alpha Kappa Alpha Sorority, Inc., Phi Epsilon Omega Chapter.*

Alpha Kappa Alpha Sorority, Inc., Phi Epsilon Omega Chapter. November 18, 2012, *Meeting of Alpha Kappa Alpha Sorority, Inc., Phi Epsilon Omega Chapter.*

Alpha Kappa Alpha Sorority, Inc., Phi Epsilon Omega Chapter. September 15, 2013, *Meeting of Alpha Kappa Alpha Sorority, Inc., Phi Epsilon Omega Chapter.*

Alpha Kappa Alpha Sorority, Inc., Phi Epsilon Omega Chapter End of the year report, 2011, Program submission

Alpha Kappa Alpha Sorority, Inc., Phi Epsilon Omega Chapter End of the year report, 2012, Program submission

Alpha Kappa Alpha Sorority, Inc., Phi Epsilon Omega Chapter End of the year report, 2013, Program submission

Alpha Kappa Alpha Sorority, Inc., Phi Epsilon Omega Chapter End of the year report 2011, History, Archives report, Oral History Transcripts.

Alpha Kappa Alpha Sorority, Inc. Ivy Memoirs Album 2012, Second Century Edition, Harris Connect LLC, 2012, pp. 961, 1134, 1257.

APPENDICES

CHARTER MEMBERS

Nisa (Lisa) Johnson

Germayne (Smith) Cade

Daneen Woodard Edmond

Tanya Foucher-Weekley

Sharice (McCants) Fox

Eboni (Zamani) Gallaher

Marsha L. Golliday

LaTonya A. Gunter

Desirie K. Howard-McKay

Lisa Joe

Anjanette (Ivy) Johnson

Tina (Roberson) Kenebrew

Detra C. McClarity Reynolds

Tanya McCray

Natasha (Buckner) Peña

Bakahia Reed-Madison

Cindy N. Sanders

Theresa (Andrews) Singleton

U. Schanee Woods

OFFICERS

Ultimate Women of Pink and Green Interest Group
1997-1999

Bakahia Madison (President)

Tina Kenebrew (Vice President)

Schanee Woods (Recording Secretary)

Germayne Cade (Corresponding Secretary)

Tanya Foucher-Weekley (Treasurer)

Marsha L. Golliday (Membership Chairman)

Desirie Howard-McKay (Hostess)

Anjanette (Ivy) Johnson (Fundraising Chairman)

Cindy N. Sanders (Historian/Ivy Leaf Reporter)

Sharice Fox (Communications Chairman)

Theresa Andrews-Singleton (Bylaws Chairman)

LaTonya Gunter (Sergeant-at-Arms)

Phi Epsilon Omega Chapter
1999-2000

Bakahia Madison (Basileus)

Marsha L. Golliday (Anti-Basileus)

Anjanette Johnson (Grammateus)

Tanya Foucher-Weekley (Tamiouchos)

Germayne Cade (Epistoleus)

Theresa Andrews-Singleton (Parliamentarian)

LaTonya Gunter (Philacter)

Cindy N. Sanders (Historian)

LaTisha Bell (Hodegos)

Daneen W. Edmond (Membership Chairman)

Timeka Patton Gee (Fundraising Chairman)

Schanee Woods (Ivy Leaf Reporter)

2001-2002

Anjanette (Ivy) Johnson (Basileus)

Marsha L. Golliday (Anti-Basileus)

Bakahia Madison (2nd Anti-Basileus, 2002, Parliamentarian 2001-2002)

Germayne Cade (Grammateus)

Tanya Foucher (Tamiouchos)

Timeka Gee (Pecunious Grammateus, Graduate Advisor)

Cindy N. Sanders (Graduate Advisor)

Denedra Givens (Epistoleus)

Keiana Peyton (Ivy Leaf Reporter)

Daneen W. Edmond (Membership Chairman)

Latisha Bell (Fundraising Chairman)

Charlesnika Evans (Historian)

Kimberly White (Hodegos)

Celeste Smith (Leadership Coordinator)

LaTonya Gunter (Philacter)

2003-2004

Tanya Foucher-Weekley (Basileus)

Timeka Gee (Anti-Basileus)

Germayne Cade (2nd Anti-Basileus)

Daneen W. Edmond (Grammateus)

Breian Meakens (Tamiouchos)

Cindy N. Sanders (Pecunious Grammateus)

Bakahia Madison (Graduate Advisor)

Keiana Peyton (Epistoleus)

Latisha Bell (Ivy Leaf Reporter)

Charlesnika Evans (Membership Chairman)

Rachel Rowell (Fundraising Chairman)

Antoinette Patton (Historian)

Deana Sanders 2003, Lakeisha Ross 2004 (Hodegos)

Celeste Smith (Leadership Coordinator, Chaplain)

Marsha L. Golliday (Standards Chairman, Parliamentarian)

LaTonya Gunter (Nominating Chairman)

Sharice Fox (Philacter)

2005-2006

Daneen W. Edmond (Basileus)

Timeka Patton Gee (Anti-Basileus)

Celeste Smith (2nd Anti-Basileus, Chaplain, Webmistress)

Tanya Foucher (Grammateus, Parliamentarian)

Breian Meakens (Tamiouchos)

Kamita Terrell (Pecunious Grammateus)

Katrina Terrell (Epistoleus)

Bakahia Madison (Graduate Advisor)

Nikki Wilson (Ivy Leaf Reporter)

Charlesnika Evans (Membership Chairman)

Keiana Peyton (Fundraising Chairman)

Sukari Washington (Hodegos)

LaKeisha Grace-Stewart (Leadership Coordinator)

Cindy N. Sanders (Standards Chairman)

Lisa Sargent (Scholarship Coordinator)

Rachel Rowell (Historian)

Detra McClarity Reynolds (Philacter)

2007-2008

Timeka Gee (Basileus)

Germayne Cade (Anti-Basileus)

Tamara McClain (2nd Anti-Basileus)

Charlesnika Evans (Grammateus)

Kamita Terrell (Tamiouchos)

Katrina Terrell (Pecunious Grammateus)

LaTonya Gunter (Epistoleus)

Cindy N. Sanders (Graduate Advisor)

Tonya Weatherly (Ivy Leaf Reporter)

Yolanda Talley (Membership Chairman)

Ceshia Wilder (Fundraising Chairman)

Lisa Sargent (Hodegos, Scholarship Coordinator)

Denedra Givens (Leadership Coordinator)

Daneen W. Edmond (Standards Chairman, Parliamentarian)

Bakahia Madison (Historian)

Celeste Smith (Chaplain, Webmistress)

Tanya Foucher-Weekley (EAF Captain)

Shawanda Jennings (Nominating Chairman)

Marsha L. Golliday (Philacter)

2009-2010

LaTonya Gunter (Basileus)

Tamara McClain (Anti-Basileus)

Katrina Terrell (2nd Anti-Basileus)

Toya Campbell (Grammateus)

Kamita Terrell (Tamiouchos)

Ceshia Wilder (Pecunious Grammateus)

Attiyya Williams (Epistoleus)

Sharice Fox (Graduate Advisor)

Charlesnika Evans (Ivy Leaf Reporter)

Antoinette Weston (Membership Chairman)

Michelle Rainey (Fundraising Chairman)

De'Onna Cavin (Hodegos)

Shawanda Jennings (Standards Chairman)

Timeka Gee (Parliamentarian)

Antoinette Patton (Historian)

Tonya Williams (Chaplain)

Shivonne Sims (Philacter)

2011-2012

Tamara McClain (Basileus)

Cindy N. Sanders (Anti-Basileus)

Michelle Rainey (2nd Anti-Basileus)

Shawanda Jennings (Grammateus)

Ceshia Wilder (Tamiouchos)

Sandra Rush-Atkins (Pecunious Grammateus)

Lori Burns (Epistoleus)

Sharice Fox (Graduate Advisor)

Hareder McDowell (Ivy Leaf Reporter)

Detra McClarity Reynolds (Membership Chairman)

De'Onna Cavin (Fundraising Chairman)

Attiyya Williams (Hodegos)

Daneen W. Edmond (Standards Chairman)

Bakahia Madison (Parliamentarian)

Nicole Spicer (Scholarship Coordinator)

Germayne Cade (Historian)

Tonya Weatherly (Chaplain)

LaTonya Gunter (EAF Captain)

Yolanda Talley (Nominating Chairman)

Marsha L. Golliday (Philacter)

2013-2014

Cindy N. Sanders (Basileus)

Shawanda Jennings (Anti-Basileus)

Attiyya Williams (2nd Anti-Basileus)

Nicole Spicer (Grammateus)

Ceshia Wilder (Tamiouchos)

Sandra Rush-Atkins (Pecunious Grammateus)

Ursula Burns (Epistoleus)

Barbara Martin (Graduate Advisor)

Alicia Mattocks (Ivy Leaf Reporter)

Detra McClarity Reynolds (Membership Chairman)

Hareder McDowell (Fundraising Chairman)

Tamara McClain (Hodegos)

Antoinette Patton (Standards Chairman)

Bakahia Madison (Parliamentarian)

Lori Burns (Scholarship Coordinator)

Yolanda Talley (Historian)

Tammy Scott-Brand (Chaplain)

Ursula Burns (EAF Captain)

Shivonne Sims (Connection Chairman)

Daneen W. Edmond (Technology Chairman)

Sharice Fox (Philacter)

2013/2014 PHI EPSILON OMEGA CHAPTER MEMBERS

Lori Burns, Eta Tau 1989

Ursula Burns, Zeta Iota 1988

Javanese Byrd, Phi Epsilon Omega, 2013

Germayne Cade, Lambda Tau Omega 1996

Toya L. Campbell, Zeta Iota 1991

De'Onna Cavin, Phi Epsilon Omega 2006

Christine Chambers, Zeta Iota, 2005

Marian Dozier, General, 1992

Daneen W. Edmond, Theta Rho Omega 1993

Charlesnika Evans, Phi Epsilon Omega 2000

Tanya Foucher-Weekley, Zeta Iota 1991

Sharice Fox, Lambda Tau Omega 1996

Timeka Patton Gee, Pi Nu 1998

Marsha L. Golliday, Zeta Iota 1991

Shawn L. Govan, Zeta Iota 1988

Danielle Graham-Harris, Zeta Iota 1988

Denedra Grossett, Zeta Iota, 1997

LaTonya Gunter, Zeta Iota 1990

Rhea Henderson, Zeta Iota 1989

Shawanda Jennings, Phi Epsilon Omega 2007

Nisa Johnson, Zeta Iota 1989

Tina C. Kenebrew, Zeta Iota 1990

Amissah Lemieux-Seals, Phi Epsilon Omega 2013

Bakahia Madison, Zeta Iota 1991

Barbara Martin, Zeta Iota 1989

Alicia Mattocks, Zeta Iota 1985

Tamara McClain, Nu Omicron Omega 2004

Hareder McDowell, Zeta Iota 2003

LaKeisha McGee, Phi Epsilon Omega 2000

Brittany McGhee, Phi Epsilon Omega 2013

Catherine Amy Moy, Phi Epsilon Omega 2013

Antoinette Patton, Lambda Psi 1992

Jeanne Pierce, Phi Epsilon Omega 2013

Michelle Rainey, Phi Epsilon Omega 2006

Sherry Randall-Hardin, Zeta Iota 1981

Detra McClarity Reynolds, Lambda Tau Omega 1996

Trina Robinson, Phi Epsilon Omega 2013

Sandra Rush-Atkins, Phi Epsilon Omega 2007

Cindy N. Sanders, Lambda Tau Omega 1996

Lisa Sargent-Davis, Phi Epsilon Omega 2000

Tammy Scott-Brand, Zeta Iota 1988

Monica Shirley, Phi Epsilon Omega 2013

Shivonne Sims, Phi Epsilon Omega 2000

Nicole Spicer, Zeta Iota 2001

Dana Stafford-Menefee, Zeta Iota 1984

Dana Stamps-Woods, Zeta Iota 2003

Yolanda Talley, Phi Epsilon Omega 2000

Kamita Terrell, Phi Epsilon Omega 2002

Katrina Terrell, Phi Epsilon Omega 2002

Maji Tharpe, Gamma 1992

Tonya Weatherly, Beta 2001

Antoinette Weston, Phi Epsilon Omega 2006

Ceshia Wilder, Phi Epsilon Omega 2006

Attiyya Williams, Phi Epsilon Omega 2006

Nikki Wilson, Phi Epsilon Omega 2002

Dianne Wolfe, Phi Epsilon Omega 2013

U. Schanee Woods, Zeta Iota 1989

PHI EPSILON OMEGA CHAPTER SORORS OF THE YEAR

Bakahia Madison	2000 (Awarded in 2001)
Timeka Patton Gee	2001 (Awarded in 2002)
Tanya Foucher-Weekley	2002 (Awarded in 2003)
Rachel Rowell	2003 (Awarded in 2004)
Charlesnika Evans	2004 (Awarded in 2005)
Daneen W. Edmond	2005 (Awarded in 2006)
Lisa Sargent	2006 (Awarded in 2007)
Germayne Cade	2008
Tamara McClain	2009
Sharice Fox	2010
Sandra Rush-Atkins	2011
Antoinette Patton	2012
Hareder McDowell	2013

UNSUNG SHEROES

Bakahia Madison 2007

Timeka Patton Gee 2008

Tanya Foucher-Weekley 2009

REGIONAL AWARDS

Chapter attendance for small chapter, 67th Central Regional Conference

Outstanding Basileus, 72nd Central Regional Conference

CONFERENCE HOST

75th Central Regional Conference (with Phi Kappa Omega)

INDEX

Made in United States
Orlando, FL
29 March 2025